The Way He Made Me Feel

From the Memoirs of
Tatiana Y. Thumbtzen

Co-Authored by
Tonia Ryan

WII
Books

Photography Credits
Page 3, 166 by Richard Armais; page 10, 14, 165, 176 by Jim Maxwell; page 22 by Eddie Cole: page 24 by Mom & Dad; page 28 by Mom; page 29, 30 by Barry Lategan; Mike Reinhardt page 34, page 67, 88 by Julie Ellis: page 69 by Dad; page 73 by Sam Emerson; page 85 by Angela Alvarado; page 170, 175 by Greg Gorman; page 137 by Demetrie Kabbaz; page 181 by Luis Gomez; page 184, 187 by Rich Jackson; page 188 by Christopher Ameruoso.
All other photographs courtesy of the author.

The Way He Made Me Feel

Jacket design by Tatiana Y. Thumbtzen
Jacket Graphic Design by Bob Newman
Backcover painting by Eric Tryus
Graphics and Illustrations designed by Tonia Ryan
Copy-Edited by Tonia Ryan

Library of Congress Cataloging-In-Publication Data
Thumbtzen, Y. Tatiana
The Way He Made Me Feel: Tatiana Y. Thumbtzen
Co-Authored by Tonia Ryan – 1st edition
ISBN 0-9763164-0-4

To Joseph
With much Love.

I dedicate this book to my Savior, The Lord Jesus Christ.
Thank you for all my blessings and the many lesson's
you put before me.
My greatest love and gratitude to you.

Table of Contents

Acknowledgements

To my parents O'Cain & Evelyn Thumbtzen-

My first set of "Guardian Angels." Thank you for all the years you have shown me love and support. Thank you for making me the person that I am today! All my love to you.

To Valerie Simpson-

I thank you so much for being you, and being there for me when I needed it. You will always be my guardian angel on earth. I cherish and love you very much. I will never forget all that you endured with me and everything that you did for me. Thank you L.A Mommy!

To my brother Harold aka (T1) and Sookhi Thumbtzen-

I thank you both for believing in me and for going that extra mile. I love you both so much and I could not have done this with out you. Thanks for your love, support, and laughs. Sookhi, Oute alofa iaoe uso! Faafetai.

To all my brother's and sisters-

I thank you for all the love and laughter shared.

To Tonia Ryan (T3) -

God bless you! I thank God for bringing you into my life everyday. I believe you are a kindred sprit who was intended to come into my life when you did. You have been a true blessing, and I look forward to the many projects' we have yet to bring into fruition. You are my outlet in which to speak and to shine. Thank you for being such a wonderful human being, and believing in me.

To Daddy D and Sucker D -

aka "Derek Cavan" and "Derek Ryan Cavan II" – Thanks to the both of you for allowing your mommy to work so hard and live on the computer for my project. Much love!

To Karen Tyrus -

Thank you for being the rock I needed to lean on sometimes. The loss of your son has been my greatest pain in this lifetime. I love you!

To Demetrie Kabbaz –

Thank you for your love, support, and inspiration. I love you Uncle D!

To all my friends –

Thank you for all your love, support, laughs, and inspiration. Tiffany Deal, Audra and Mario Oseguera, Angela and Rob Rosa, Christopher Ameruoso, Elie Rodriquez, Rich Hill, Omar Alberto, Jerry Perez, Kelly Curry, Greg Clark , Iris Parker, Eddie DeHarp, Marie and Chris Dale, Marie Gabriel, Bernard Fowler, Diane Gordon, Nathasha Raganoonan, Freddy Hernandez, Lerlin Martinez, Brittany Ervin, Randy Pfund, and last but not least - Luis (Wicked) Gomez

To Mr. Magic Michael (my cat) -

Thanks for all your unconditional love and purrs. You have been my best friend. You deserve my acknowledgment after being by my side through the good and bad thirteen year's later. I wub u! I love you too Chica, even though you are a brat!

To Joseph:
Tonia

Foreword

My name is Tonia Ryan and I am Tatiana's webmaster, co-author, manager, business partner, and her friend. Tatiana and I have been working on these projects, especially this book, since October of 2002. When I met Tatiana, it seemed to me that she decided to give up on following her dreams. I was getting a divorce, and I did not want to start a new project. Something brought us together for a reason. I had been working extremely hard for years straight and I just finally wanted some time for me. It was time for me to have some fun! I decided to move to South Beach, Florida. People go to South Beach for many reasons. Not only does this coastal community have incredible restaurants, awesome nightclubs, and the best designer shops, I think it is the most beautiful beach in Florida. My plans were to enjoy life spending my savings, relax, and have a great time. I wanted a stress free lifestyle.

I moved into a beautiful condominium on Collins Avenue with an outstanding ocean view. I had a daily routine that I followed. I started each day at the gym which was conveniently located within the high-rise. Afterwards, I walked to a new restaurant on 16th and Collins Ave. I had been to a few of their other restaurants in California and they were incredibly popular, so I hoped this one was as fun as the others. It was, and before I knew it, I turned the counter bar into my "office" – combining my meals with phone calls on various projects. I became close friends with Greg Clark, the bartender who waited on me daily. One day he approached me and asked, "What exactly do you mean when you say you are a webmaster? Does that have to do with the Internet?" I explained to him that I attended UNLV in Las Vegas and that I build websites, create graphics, and edit video. I work on everything related to the web and a web site. Greg did not even own a computer so he did not understand much of what I was telling him. "You need to talk to my friend Tatiana," said Greg. "She is a hostess here and she needs a website. She used to work with Michael Jackson, you know. She was in that *Thriller* video I think. I'm not sure. It was one of his videos. I can't remember, but I am going to tell her about you." I laughed, enjoying his enthusiasm but answered him directly. "I am not taking on any new projects right now, but I will give her some information that will help her out."

A few days later, I met Tatiana for lunch at "my barside office." I was determined to find out as much as I could about her because I did not recognize her from any of Michael Jackson's videos. I knew that she was not the young woman from the *Thriller* video because I was ten years old when that video came out and I must have seen it a thousand times. Therefore, I knew what the young woman looked like and this was not the person I was sitting across from. Tatiana told me that she had appeared in the video, *The Way You Make Me Feel,* which was released in 1988. I was in my senior year of high school and I was not watching Michael Jackson videos. I was into *The Beastie Boys, 2 Live Crew, and Suicidal Tendencies*. I told Tatiana that I did not remember ever seeing the video, and she seemed surprised. She said, "You have to have seen the video. I think everyone has seen that video." I replied, "Maybe I did, but I am sure that I changed the channel when it came on." I then explained to her that I did not want to sound rude, but I was only seventeen years old at the time. Michael Jackson was not cool to my friends and me. We grew out of that stage a longtime ago. She later gave me a copy of the video and then I remembered how much the music television stations played that video. She was right! Everyone had seen that video! Myself included.

Tatiana explained that she had studied ballet and had been a professional model for years before the infamous video. My question was how she went from superstar status to a hostess at a restaurant. Not that I think there is anything wrong with being a hostess, I just became more intrigued with her fascinating story. Tatiana explained that the last major job that she had was being on tour with Michael Jackson after the huge success of the video release. I wondered how someone with so much, with such exposure from the video, be without work in her industry. For most people, the video would be the beginning of a career, not the end of one. I realized that if I am this interested in her life, the people who have followed her career had to be very interested in what had become of this beautiful, talented young woman. It was then that we decided to work together to tell her story.

Tatiana and I "hung out" with each other everyday for the next few months. We had dinner at a different five star restaurant almost every night and I dragged her with me to all the South Beach and Miami hot spots. I wanted to find out as much as I could about her before I started working on our project. I also loved having a friend to share the fun of South Beach. Tatiana and I quickly became close friends. We had a blast! I felt she needed to have some fun now, as much as I did. We learned a lot about each other.

Before I become a business partner with someone, I want to know as much as I possibly can about them, personally and professionally. Being business partners is like a marriage in many ways. I asked Tatiana one night, "What is most important to you when you think about this project? What is your number one reason that you want to write a book?" Tatiana replied, "Tonia, I never got the chance to tell my story in my own words." Several books and tabloids had published misquotes stating they were Tatiana's words but they always changed her words or used them out of context. I promised her that I would not change one word of her story. For the next two years, I worked at co-writing her book while keeping her words true to her memory, her thoughts, and her feelings. Tatiana shared her diary with me which was the key to helping me keep my commitment and meet the most challenging aspect of this project. After several rewrites, I thought the best way for the reader to have a feel for Tatiana's life and her experiences would be to publish Tatiana's diary the way she had written it. Staying true to her original format, I decided to interview her myself. That way, it would be Tatiana's words taking us on the journey through her own eyes. *The Way He Made Me Feel* is finally "the real story!"

Introduction

By Tatiana Y. Thumbtzen

The Way He Made Me Feel is a book about the portion of my life when I lived in Hollywood, Ca. I invite you to my journey from my life as a little girl and all the dreams I had and continue to deeply believe in. Who would have thought that someday they could all come true? I believe everything in life does have a reason and a purpose. Fate and destiny do exist, and my story proves this true. My journey chronicles my personal love of dance from the tender age of six, to becoming a prodigy of Violette Verdy; a prima ballerina of the famous choreographer George Balanchine. During my stint as a model in New York City and in Japan, the legendary Barry Lategan "scouted me out." He was the fashion world's acclaimed photographer having discovered Twiggy in the 60's. I then furthered my journey, and Antonio Lopez took me under his wing. He had discovered the memorable talents of Jerry Hall, Jessica Lange, Pat Cleveland and Grace Jones. For all of this was the beginning of new horizons for me and lead me closer to my road of fate.

On the way to an audition in 1984, who did I find pounding the pavement of New York City – a mere five feet in front of me? Mr. Michael Jackson! The King of Pop! The "Bad" one, from the *Bad Tour* of course, and the one I had admired, idolized, and dreamt about as a small child. Nine years later, this memory gave me something to talk about when I was cast to co-star in the music video, *The Way You Make Me Feel*. It was then that my career leapt to its next plateau, and "Hollywood called."

After only a year in the land of dreams and lost angels, the ultimate dream of dreams came true. I believe that what you want in life wants you too. However, I had no idea that on August 29, 1987, what began as my dream would ultimately become my nightmare. I now realize that when you are blessed, you may be a cursed as well. As part of the Michael Jackson tour my face and image were used on several of the promotional items such as the 45 single and calendars. I was never compensated for these sales and it was then I also learned the mistakes being made by people on my own team. As these issues were exposed, a concerned call from Michael's parents enticed me into a management contract that was to fulfill my hopes (and their promises) that they were going to research and clear up the issue that I had been treated unprofessionally. Most important, I wanted to know why I had not been compensated for the use of my likeness. Time passed and no one had answers for me. Then suddenly, job offers stopped coming my way. I began to wonder if the rumors were right; maybe I was being blackballed from the industry. I began to feel that I was being watched and I knew I was being controlled and manipulated. I later learned that it was so much more.

Because I was graced with my newfound fame, the fame brought other experiences with powerful showbiz entities that continued to reveal themselves. Still, as disappointing as all of these experiences would turn out to be, none of them mystified or hurt me as much as my dream man did. My dreams forced me to open my eyes and see more than I could ever have imagined. For it was time for me to wake up and see the truth, for what it was; the truth that others tried desperately to have me see.

Opposite and page 18: The original memoirs

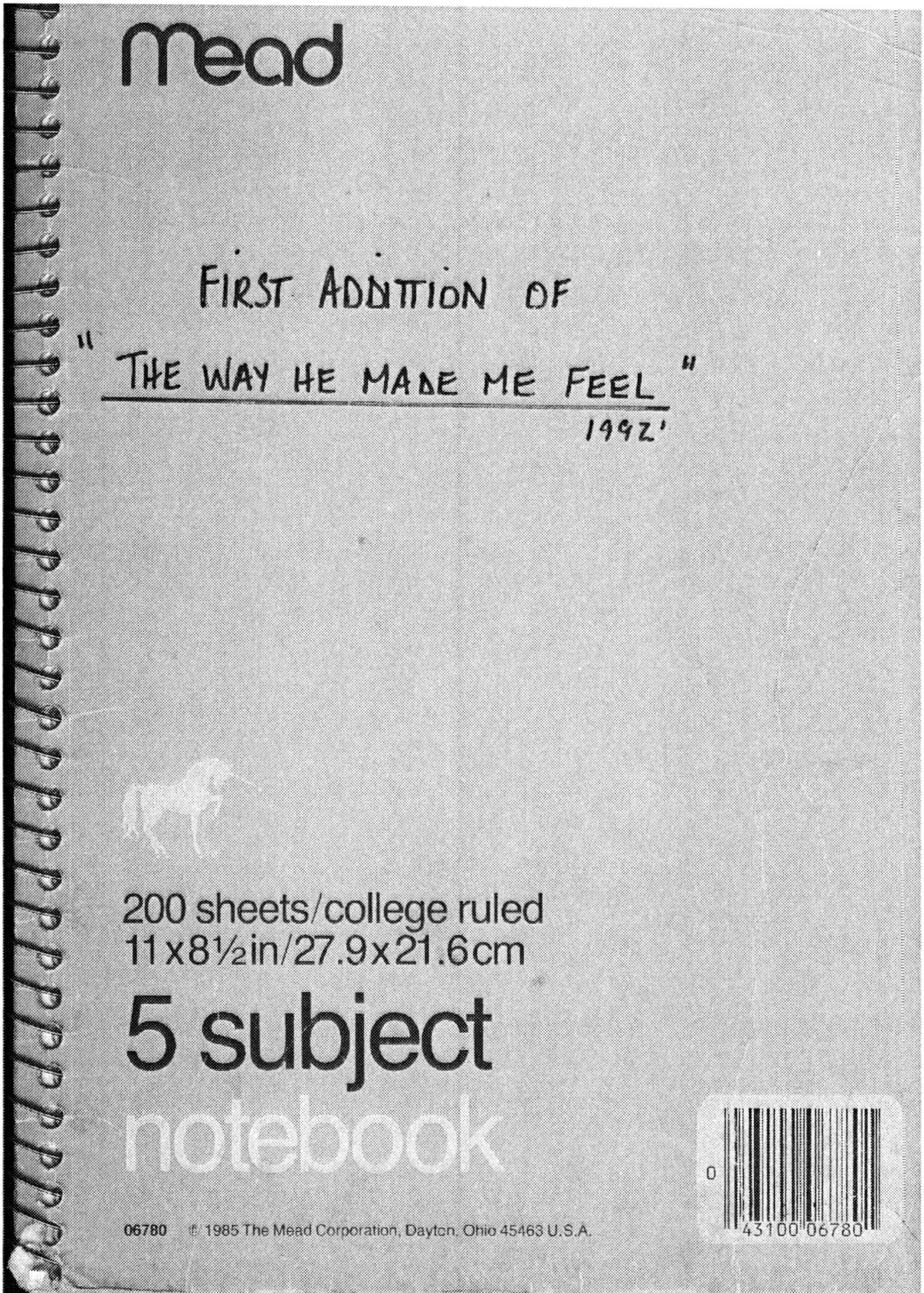
Mead
FIRST ADDITION OF
" THE WAY HE MADE ME FEEL "
1992'
200 sheets/college ruled
11x8½in/27.9x21.6cm
5 subject
notebook
06780 © 1985 The Mead Corporation, Dayton, Ohio 45463 U.S.A.
0 43100 06780

Stuart Hall
SECOND ADDITION OF
"THE WAY HE MADE ME FEEL"
1992
3 SUBJECT DIVIDED
THEMEBOOK
120 SHEETS • 11 IN. x 8½ IN.
COLLEGE RULE • NO. 4386
0 71723 41850 2
STUART HALL CO., INC.
KANSAS CITY, MO 64108, USA

Diary Excerpt

March 1993

The year of 1987 was one of the most memorable years of my life. I could never have dreamed that the year would be a major turning point in my life and my career. To some people, I was the luckiest girl in the world. However, with everything good came the bad. The true irony was the album and the tour was entitled "BAD." Looking back, that name holds real meaning to me because, unfortunately, the *Bad Tour* was filled with painful memories. It was a confusing period in my life and in my career. Working with Michael Jackson was a dream come true for me. As a ballet student, I often fantasized about dancing with him. Three or four years prior to being cast in *The Way You Make Me Feel* video, I was modeling in Miami and Japan. Dawn, one of my closest friends from home once said, "You know you should go to Los Angeles someday and try to meet Michael Jackson. I bet you'd work together and he would probably love you." We lost touch since then but I have always wondered what her thoughts were after seeing the video. It was such an unexpected thought and really, a premonition of what was to come.

Through the years, the more Michael's face "changed," the more people compared me to him. I always found humor in those comments and I always found myself correcting them. How do you compare the face someone was born with to someone who has chosen to reconstruct their 'signature' to the world; their face?

Not that I felt that these comparisons were an insult, but I also never felt they were a compliment. My parents raised me to believe that we are all original so I always felt funny when people compared me to someone who has surgically altered himself or herself repeatedly. Then there are those who stated their feelings more bluntly and said, "He probably chose you for the video because Michael sees himself in you." That could be and probably is, one of the truest statements. It was at one time anyway. I do think when Michael saw the videotape of my audition for *The Way You Make Me Feel* video, in someway, he saw in me a mirror image of a look he had been cultivating for years. Therefore, to be honest, I stumbled across luck and perhaps my mere fate. I am not selling myself short. The strenuous audition process proved that talent was necessary and I believe my personality worked to my advantage in landing the role.

At the age of eight, I wrote Michael a letter that I slaved over for days. I put a lot of thought into it, correcting the spelling and my topics. I even had a photo of myself picked out to enclose with this letter. Then I finally decided the letter would never reach him or that he would not care, so I put it in my wastebasket. I never sent it! During this time, I nagged my mother for a Jackson 5 album. The *ABC* album was very popular, and I guess like every kid in America, I played it to death. When I met Michael, I never mentioned the letter or the dreams I had as a young girl.

Opposite: This was the picture I was going to send to MJ with my letter. I was eight years old

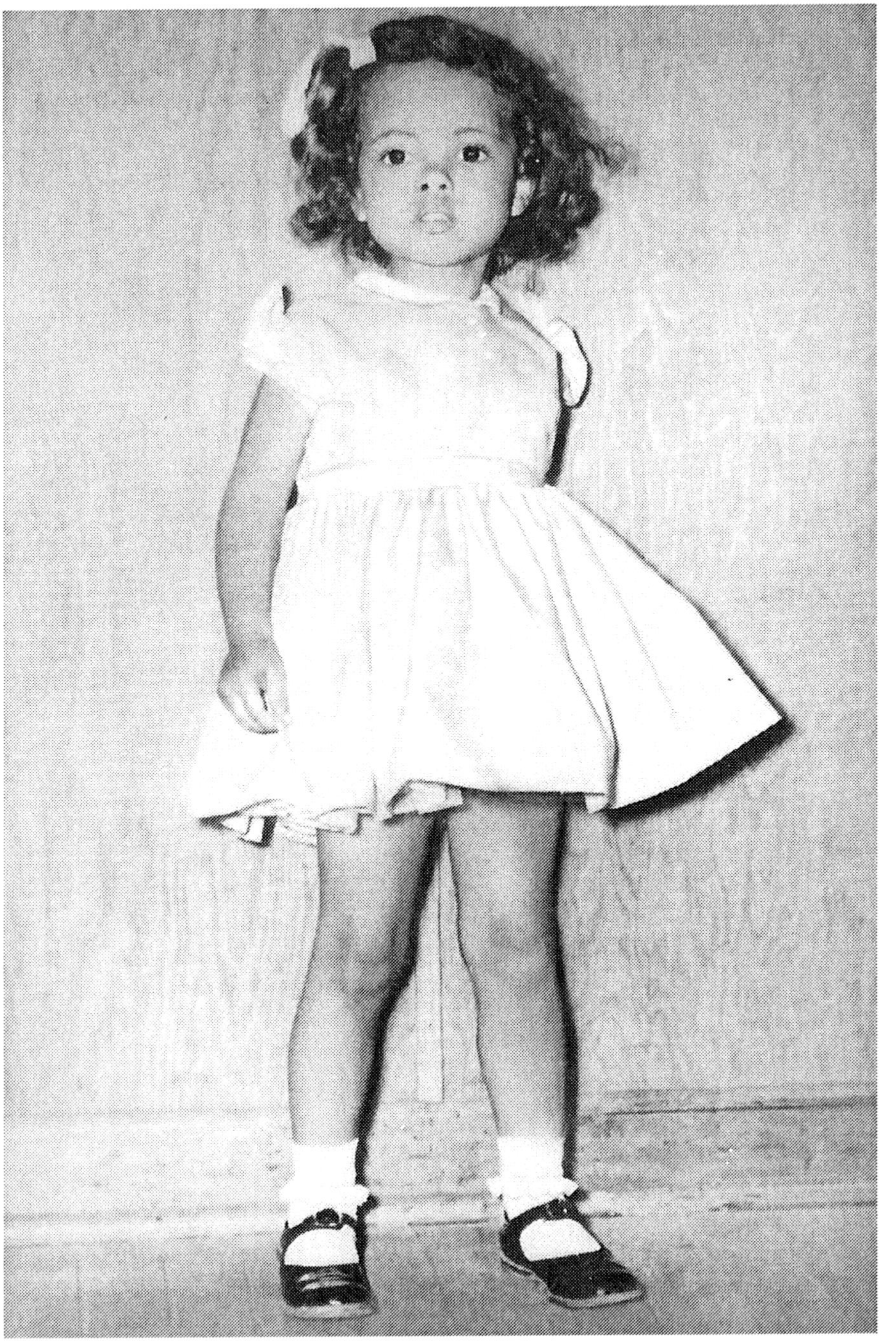

Me when I was four years old

Chapter One
In The Beginning

Tonia Ryan **(TR)**

Tatiana, let's start from the beginning. Where were you born?

Tatiana Thumbtzen **(TT)**

I was born in Clearwater, on the gulf coast of Florida. Clearwater is adjacent to Tampa, home of the Tampa Bay Buccaneers – the Superbowl champs of 2002.

TR: What is your family like?

TT: My parents, O'Cain and Evelyn Thumbtzen were both teachers. My father was a principal and my mother was an art teacher. They are my adoptive parents, but as far as I am concerned, they will always be my true family, for better or for worse. My parents came from a melting pot of cultures that include Irish, Black, and Native American Indian. The family name is of German decent. I have two older brothers, Harold who is the comedian; and William is the train fanatic. My older sister Pamela is the animal lover. They were already out of the house and on their own when I came along so it was like I was the only child. I also have three half siblings and I choose to protect their identity and privacy.

TR: What was it like having both parents who were teachers?

TT: It was not easy. Discipline ruled in our household. Deep down, part of me felt guilty for loathing school when my parents were both teachers. But I still hated school. It was impossible to concentrate and to not hate school when I was always being picked on. I couldn't figure out why the kids were harassing me or why I seemed to be "the oddball."

Me with my Mom and Dad on Christmas 77-78

I was eventually told why I was being taunted; the black kids treated me the worst. One of them shoved me against a wall. She was a large black girl who was making my life a living hell. She told me, "You ain't black, you ain't white, what color you is anyway? I bet you do not even know!" When I replied, "I'm the color you see I am," she hated that answer! After those words came rushing out of my mouth, I prepared myself to die. Although the words flew freely out of my mouth, I had spoken with confidence. To my shock and pleasant surprise, my bully simply walked away mumbling, "You think you're smart ass." I was telling the truth. I was not trying to be a smart ass at all. She asked me what color I was, not what race. I come from a family of educators and we call it heritage or background. To me, color meant pigment not race.

That experience opened my eyes to the differences in people for the first time. I noticed the kids at my school were either black or white. I was the oddball! I learned the black kids hated that I was so close to looking white. The girls especially hated it. I guess they felt I could pass for white if I wanted to. The white kids did not seem to care. They found my heritage interesting. I am a mixture of Cherokee Indian, Black, and Cuban. In short, I am an American. I am the girl next door.

Unfortunately, there were more bullies to come. One, named Michelle, lived down the street from us. She was a pretty girl but was on the heavy side. I was small and petite. One of the neighborhood boys told me that they voted me the "prettier one." I tried being her friend, but it was obvious she preferred hating me instead.

TR: Were your parents strict with you?

TT: Being the "baby" still at home, my parents spoiled and overprotected me. I hated the overprotection. At one point, I could only ride my bike on the driveway of our home. I was relieved when I finally graduated and was able to ride it to the end of the street and back. This was total freedom. I could not understand my parent's nonstop worry and concern for me. However, I do understand it today. So many kids have parents who do not even care. The way I see it, caring too much is better than not caring at all.

TR: When you were a child, did you feel that there was something special about you?

TT: I was four years old the first time I can remember making an impression on someone; I remember it like it was yesterday. I had Shirley Temple like curls in my hair. I was so embarrassed once, when a friend of my mothers made a big deal about how cute I looked. She was oooohing and ahhhhing over me. I cringed with shyness because of the attention and I hid behind my mothers' dress. Thank God for that dress, I thought. I remember hating that this woman was so focused on me, and yet I thought, wow, all of this attention for me?

TR: Can you remember a specific gift you received as a child?

TT: Yes, The very first gift I remember my mother giving me was a pair of black patent leather shoes, with a little strap going across the front. They were so shiny that they just sparkled. They were like magical shoes to me and when I received them I remember asking "These are for me?" I also remember Mom dressing me like a little doll in frilly dresses with ruffles and bows. I even had ruffles on the bottom of my underwear. Of course, what I really wanted was to dress like my sister Pam. She was a tomboy and always wore jeans and T-shirts. What we remember from our childhood often sets the pace for our mental health and determines our outcome as adults. In my case, there was always this underlying feeling that I was a bit different and did not always fit in. I was a kid who grew up in my own fantasy world. I daydreamed in my classes, where I drew pictures of ballerinas and horses.

TR: Did your parents let you watch television as a child?

TT: Television played a big part in my fantasies and dreams. I lost myself in movies like *Singing in the Rain*, with Gene Kelley, and *The Wizard of Oz*. The musicals enthralled me. Everyone in them just seemed so happy. My favorite performers were Lena Horn, Rita Hayworth, and Dorothy Dandridge. To me, these were incredible women. *The Ed Sullivan Show* was also a favorite in our household and brought classical ballet into my life.

When I was six, I watched one of the Sullivan shows and I laid eyes on Violett Verdy and Edward Villela. I was in awe. Their dancing was the most beautiful and magical movements I had ever seen. I cried and pleaded, "Mommy, Mommy, I want to do that! I want to be a ballerina." My Mom bought me a children's book on ballet. I soaked up every page, position, and dance term. I mimicked and practiced ballet positions constantly. I lived for anything and everything that had to do with ballet, music, and dance.

When the Jackson Five made their first appearance on the show, I knew I loved not only their music but also the smallest one named, Michael. When I watched him perform for the first time, I thought he was the greatest performer that I had ever seen. His talent amazed me and he was cute too! Diana Ross and The Supremes introduced The Jackson 5 for another television appearance and I decided that Diana Ross and The Supremes were it for me too. Diana's look was striking and different.

When I turned eight years old, I was able to enroll in a local ballet Academy that was operated by Beatriz De Paris, a teacher of *The Balenchine Technique*.

TR: Did you make friends in dance class?

TT: In dance class, I met my first friend, Marion. I had everything in common with her. We were even the same age. Although ballet was taking a precedent in my life, I did not forget how much I loved The

Jackson 5 and its youngest member. It was during the release of the single *Ben* that I slaved over that letter I intended to send to Michael. I wrote repeatedly, balling up pieces of paper that I kept throwing on the floor.

TR: Did you enjoy ballet?

TT: Yes, I went on point early —at age ten. It usually takes a couple of years before you go on your toes but I was ready and could not wait to do so. This was also a childhood dream of mine.

TR: Did you want to pursue ballet as a career?

TT: My idol Violette Verdy, whom I had seen on *The Ed Sullivan Show* visited our school and pointed out Marion and me as the top students. Violette said, "They have great talent and potential. I will follow their work and progress closely." She kept her promise and returned two years later offering both of us an opportunity of a lifetime. She offered us the chance to study at *The School of American Ballet* - the training camp for the famous *New York City Ballet Company*.

TR: How old were you when Violette invited you to *The School of American Ballet?*

TT: In 1973, I was thirteen years old. I traveled to New York City with my mother. I was awestruck and excited to say the least. In addition to my classes, I studied with several of the greatest Russian dancers of our time. Alexandra Danilova was one of my teachers. One day on my way to class, my mother and I were approached by an agent asking if my mom would allow me to do some work as an "extra" on a film. The film was *Taxi Driver* with Robert DeNiro, whom I met years later. I was disappointed when my Mother decided to pass on the opportunity but I got over it quickly when my idol, Violett, told us that I had been offered a full scholarship to *The School of American Ballet* at Julliard. The most prestigious art school in the country.

TR: How did you feel when that happened?

TT: This was it! My dream was coming true! A woman I had admired and idolized as a child and had seen *on The Ed Sullivan Show* was now hand picking me and taking me under her wing as her protégé. Talk about major changes in my little life. I believed wholeheartedly in every dream and vision I had. Never did I feel anything was unattainable or impossible. My parents also encouraged me and told me that anything was possible with hard work and diligence. When we returned to Clearwater, my mom and dad had some serious lengthy discussions about my future and the choices they were about to make.

TR: So did they decide to let you go to New York?

TT: Yes, in the end my dreams and love for ballet won. I moved in with Violette and her mother on Eighty-Fifth Street and West End Avenue. They took care of me and the other handpicked girls who attended the school. We lived in a penthouse. Cicely Tyson occupied the only other penthouse on that floor.

Backyard Ballet at age thirteen

This was the job that changed my life and my career.

TR: Did you get to meet Cicely Tyson?

TT: I remember being too shy to speak to her at first. However, one day I found the courage and as we stood together in the elevator, I commented about how adorable her dog was. She broke my heart and crushed me as she ignored me. I was learning that this was the

"Big Apple" not Clearwater, Florida. New Yorkers can be cold hearted or standoffish. I wished they were more hospitable and friendly.

TR: Did *The School of American Ballet* teach academic classes as well as ballet?

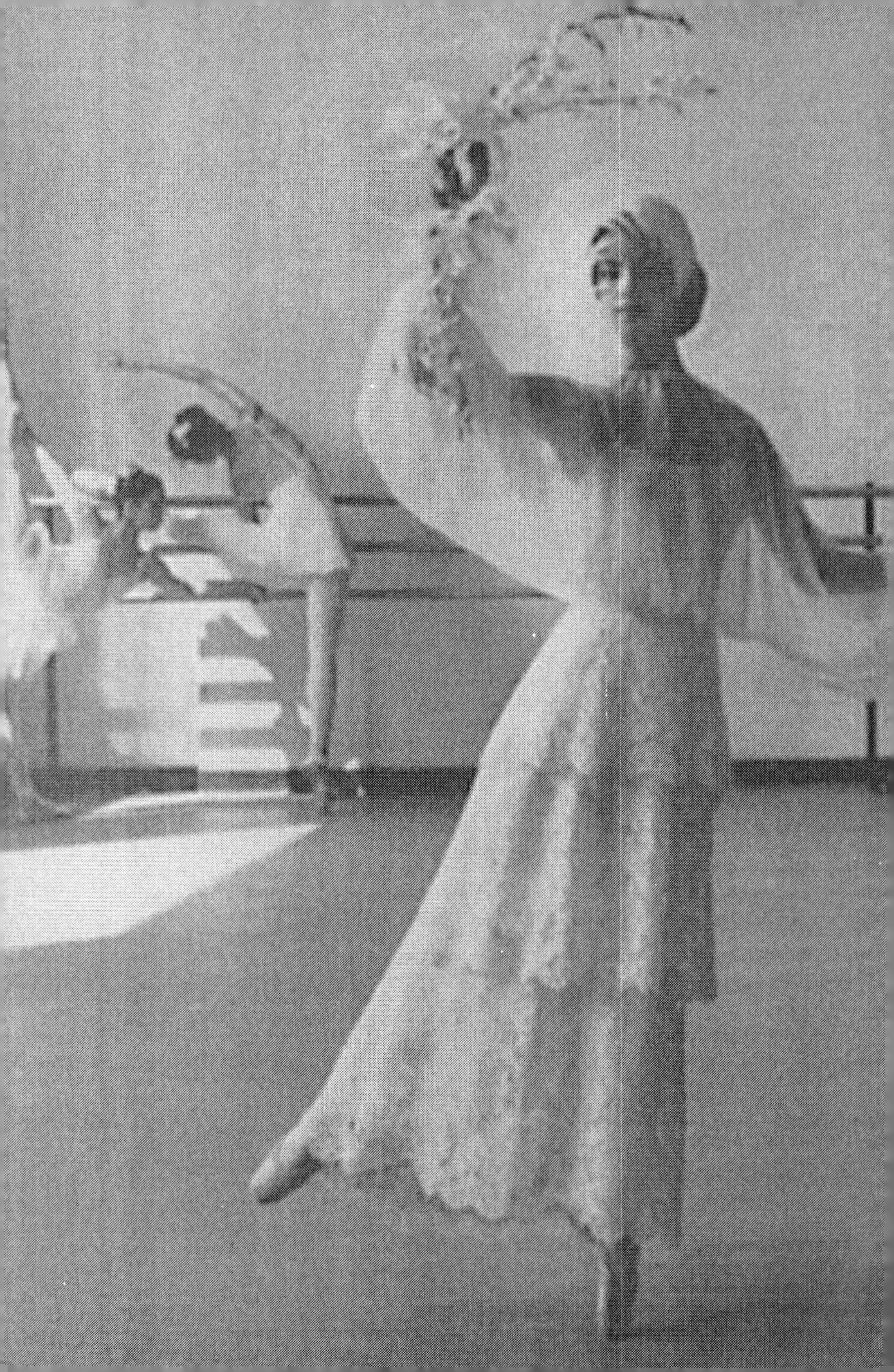

TT: Academically, I attended *The Professional Children's School.* The curriculum was designed for child stars and the wealthy kids. Some of our alumni included Christopher Walken, Uma Thurman, Phoebe Cates, and Irene Cara.

TR: Did you have the chance to meet any of your idols?

TT: Great dancers of the world often walked into the Academy and even took our classes. I remember Rudolph Nureyev, Mikhail Baryshnikov, and Natalia Makarova. My greatest idol was Gelsey Kirkland. She was a living doll to me, and she was George Balanchine's protégé. She was a prima ballerina and a principal dancer at the age of fourteen.

TR: Did you enjoy living in New York City?

TT: I loved New York. It is a multiracial and multicultural city and for the first time I fit right in. I was no longer the odd one and soon I was smitten with the commercial element of show business. While in class one day a famous photographer, Barry Lategan, was scouting dancers for a fashion layout in *Modern Bride* magazine. They chose me as one of the lucky few. Barry was the man that was famous for discovering Twiggy in the sixties. This struck a flame and tweaked my interest. The school could see there was a change in me and this did not please my mother. However, it forced me to learn something about politics and racial issues.

Mid-term, a new student arrived. She became my friend, but to my surprise, they accepted her into the company before me. Word got back that they chose her because the company needed a "token," a person of color. She was a beautiful Haitian girl of dark complexion.

TR: Why would they have chosen her when your background is part black as well?

TT: My friends told me why they chose her because there was no denying that she was black and I am a mixture of so many different races that I could be put in a variety of "racial categories." The politics of it all disturbed me. I guess you could say that I found myself rebelling against what I loved. To me, politics and race had no place in the arts. I had a

Opposite: Tatiana DANCER

lot to learn. Unfortunately, politics is in everything and is everywhere. I felt cheated, especially since I attended this school for nearly two years and when she popped up out of nowhere they chose her because of the color of her skin. It should have been based on her talent and hard work, or simply because she was their first choice.

TR: Did this change your feelings about ballet and the academy?

TT: Yes, and when people noticed my interest was changing, my friends tried to talk to me about it. The counselor of the school even tried. She promised me that they were going to invite me into the company shortly but it was already too late. I had moved on in my heart and my mind.

TR: Did you have any other interests besides ballet?

TT: I wanted to model, dance, and act. Not limit myself to being a ballerina. I was going through a lot professionally and personally. During this time, I met my first boyfriend in Central Park while on a walk with some friends one day. I was nineteen then. There he was playing Frisbee; athletically twirling and spinning through the air like a dancer. I remember being in awe of his style, his moves, and his long black hair. His name was Johnny Wilson, and he was from Chile. After meeting in the park that day, we were an item for at least a year.

TR: When did you get your first break into modeling?

TT: My first real break into the modeling world began when I met Antonio Lopez. Antonio was a famous fashion illustrator and everyone in the fashion world knew of his remarkable career. In the late 60's he discovered many well-known models. Among his clients, to name a few were: Valentino, Versace, Lagerfeld, Halston, Issey Miyake and even Bloomingdales. The models that he discovered include Jerry Hall; who he almost married, Jessica Lange, Pat Cleveland, Grace Jones and Tina Chow. Antonio's work was incredible. I just adored and cherished him. I sometimes think I even fell in love with him. However, I did not tell anyone. I waged a campaign to work with him and after five or six months of diligence and nagging; he finally gave me a break. Antonio liked my energy and he always warned me not to stop dancing. He told me it was not only my gift; he said that it separated me from the other models and that it made me stand out. After a few months of grooming, he set up a meeting for me with the *Eileen Ford Agency*, who signed me on the spot. That same day he scheduled me for a photo shoot with one of the hottest and top fashion Photographers in the business, Mike Reinhardt - whose work I admired because I 'studied' *Vogue* and *Glamour* magazines to keep up with the fashion world.

TR: How did your first modeling session go?

TT: I recall arriving at his studio and walking down a long hallway. I heard a woman's voice say aloud, "Is that Tatiana? Is that her? Is that Tatiana?" Obviously, I was curious to see who was calling my name. It was Janice Dickinson! She was the hottest model ever. She was the one I idolized and ogled over in all the magazines. She was the one I studied the most. I practiced her every pose in the mirror! I was inspired by the fact that our looks were a bit similar. At that time, I had adapted the name Tiana as my new stage name. My biological name was Stephanie and I felt the name Tiana Thumbtzen had a better ring to it. It sounded much more exotic and, I liked the "double T thing." Well, at the moment the world's first Supermodel Janice Dickinson renamed me "Tatiana Thumbtzen," I became that name! I was in awe of Janice's beauty. She was tall, thin, and exotically exquisite.

TR: Is she the Janice Dickinson who appears currently on *Americas Top Model* produced by Tyra Banks?

TT: Yes, that is her! Isn't she amazing? That day she spent some time with me between my shoot and she even gave me advice and tips about the business. I told her that I just signed with Eileen Ford and Janice was shockingly candid in her advice. "She is the wrong agent for your look. After a week, she'll dump you because she does not know how to sell you," Janice said. She advised me to seek representation with either *Zoli* or *Elite* modeling agencies. "They will understand your special exotic looks. Eileen Ford will not know what to do with you because you are not just black or just white," Janice said. I found myself flashing back to Clearwater and the torment the other kids used to put me through daily. Janice did not hold back any in telling me the agents laughed at her and complained she referred to herself as having: "Big ass lips." "Now everyone wants them!" she bragged. "They're paying me thousands for these big ass lips now," Janice laughed. I did not listen to her warning and advice. I joined *The Eileen Ford Agency* and – guess what? They dumped me at the end of that week! It broke my heart. My booker told me that I was not black enough, or I was not white enough, and that they did not know how to place me. They told me to go ahead and stick with Antonio. "He is helping you out with your career. You are better-off with him." I could not believe how right Janice was. I hated that I had not listened to her. I got the final word that I was being dropped from Ford standing in a telephone booth. I hung up the telephone in complete shock and immediately called Antonio. I was so choked up he could not understand what I was saying. He said, "Just calm down, and don't worry." He told me to grab a cab and head over to the studio. When I arrived, he put his arms around me and assured me that everything would be all right. In my mind, modeling was about beauty and not about race. Boy, did I have a lot to learn. I was still so naive about the politics of race and color.

TR: Did you contact the other modeling agencies Janice had mentioned?

TT: Before I knew it, Antonio was on the telephone and had set up a meeting for me with the *Zoli Agency.* The following day I walked into Zoli's office and they signed me on the spot. The agent told me "It is

Ford's loss and our gain to have you as a model." The best part was that Zoli sent me out and I started working immediately.

TR: What year was this?

TT: It was 1979 and before I knew it, I had a modeling contract in Japan. Overnight, I was this "new face" in the modeling world. My third job was gracing the cover of *More* magazine, which is their equivalent to *Vogue*. For the next five years, I lived and worked as a model in Tokyo, traveling constantly all over the Far East. My manager once remarked that I traveled more than the average Japanese business-person and that was saying a lot!

TR: What was it like working in a foreign country?

TT: On one of my first jobs, I traveled to a little Island named "Ito" about two hours by boat from Okinawa. The first day of shooting the photographer placed me at the chosen location. While he clicked away, I noticed that the ground beneath me felt rather hard. I knew I was standing on some foreign object and I hit it a few times with the heel of my shoe. I was trying to figure out what it was. When the photographer reloaded his film, I examined this hard object with the make-up artist standing by as we pulled away some of the surrounding shrubs. We found that I had been stomping with the heel of my shoe on an old torpedo that was left over from the days of Pearl Harbor. Can you imagine? Here I was hitting a torpedo with the heel of my shoe. I could have blown the entire crew and myself to bits — and possibly, destroyed the entire island! After the torpedo discovery, we packed up and changed our location immediately. The photographer told us that it could still detonate. It was an interesting shoot to say the least.

TR: Did you save your money when you were modeling in Japan?

TT: Antonio always told me, "Save your money Tatiana." Did I listen? Ha! That has been one of my greatest lessons in life— to listen. After five years there, I returned to New York with great memories but ready for new endeavors.

MORE
こうすれば彼もいい男になる！
あなたの生理のメカニズムを識る
●MOREの旅
スペインの熱い血潮の中で
●ファッション徹底特集
「通勤着」この夏あなたは何を着る？
モダンリビングに生きる籐家具
8

MORE
創刊3周年
Magazine「モア」
●保存版インテリア特集
ま、白い部屋がすてきだ！
新フランス料理のエスプリ
●ファッション2大特集
私のファッション・メッセージ
この夏基本となるボトムを探す
グッドカップルはベストパートナー
熱中体験！リオのカーニバル
ボーヴォワール／萩原健一
デビッド・ボウイ／イルカ
ザ・モア・リポート
アンケート募集

TR: What year did you return to New York City?

TT: I returned in 1984 and while going on one of many casting calls, who did I find pounding the pavements of New York City at just a mere five feet away from me? It was Michael Jackson! This was before he had taken on the title "The King of Pop." I could not believe it! I just could not believe my luck. I kept following him and checking him out. He dressed in jeans and a T-shirt with a cap pulled down low on his face but I could tell it was Michael Jackson. I wanted so badly to stop and talk to him but I just could not figure out what to say. I was thinking of a way to stop and talk to him. I thought that maybe I could pretend to ask him for directions, but then I thought what do I do after that? I just could not do it! I got too shy and froze at the thought of talking to him. I followed him for about five blocks before it hit me that I was going to be late for my audition. I forced myself to break out of this magical spell. I talked about this experience to my friends for weeks after that.

TR: Did you start working right away when you went back to New York?

TT: A friend of mine named D.S.T was working with the great jazz musician Herbie Hancock. D.S.T was the first "scratcher" in the hiphop world. He created a huge hit with Herbie called *Rockit* which won five awards at the 1984 *Grammys.* Herbie finished working on another song that was a follow up entitled, *Hard Rock* and he asked me to star in the video with him. This was a milestone for me. I had done plenty of commercial campaigns in Japan, but this video received international exposure.

TR: What was it like working with Herbie Hancock?

TT: It was big to me and they made me feel like a "big star." Herbie is one of the most respected artists and a legend in the jazz world. I would soon fall madly in-love with one of his band members Bernard Fowler who was the premier vocalist in his band.

TR: Did you meet any other famous people?

TT: Through Bernard, I met one of the hottest and biggest rock stars of all-time. Bernard was working late in the studio one evening and he called me and asked me to come and meet him there. I remember trying to get out of going because it was late, and I was close to going to bed but I decided to go meet him and I threw on a pair of jeans and a T-shirt. I was buzzed in, and took an elevator that opened directly into the lobby of the studio. Well, who did I find sitting before me when the elevator doors opened? He is one of the most famous faces in the world. Rock-n-Roll Royalty — Mick Jagger! I wanted to kill Bernard for surprising me like that and not telling me who was there. I did not have any make-up on and I did nothing special to prepare myself. My mother's voice echoed in my ear saying, "Always look nice when you go out, you never know whom you might meet." Mick was warm and charming. He casually said that he needed a female's voice on a part of the song that he was working on. He looked right at me when he was saying this. I had never done professional vocals, especially in a studio. I ignored his comment, because the idea of working with a rock legend frightened and intimidated me. Mick Jagger is an Icon! So, when I think about it now — I could have been on a Rolling Stones record! What a dummy I was huh? What the heck was I thinking! I deserve the "dumb ass award" for that! Nevertheless, it was a real blast just to meet him and hang out with him. Meeting Rock & Rolls "Royal Pair of Lips" was a real thrill for me. I was also so proud of Bernard for his musical accomplishments.

TR: What was your next big project in New York?

TT: A few months after the Herbie Hancock video, I made my debut in film. My friend Leon Grant had a lead roll in a film and his manager Betty Geffen took me on as a client and got me booked as an extra. The film was *Beat Street,* co-produced by the great singer Harry Belafonte and starring Rae Dawn Chong. I liked Rae Dawn's work, as I was familiar with her first film *Quest for Fire.* I felt that if she could successfully transcend beyond her exotic looks that perhaps I could too. Mr. Belafonte took a liking to me at the audition and he gave me great insight and advice on the industry. He said, "Be prepared and study hard, because they will throw you away if they can." While filming one day, he told me – like he was giving me a warning - that I stood out like a sore thumb, that I possibly attracted too much of the spotlight. His daughter Gina wondered why he took such interest in me. Gina even asked me, "What did my father say to you?" This was after we had spoken at one point. It seemed that I was threatening to her but in my head; I was thinking there was room for all of us. Mr. Belafonte asked me if I knew of any singers, gospel especially. That opened the floodgates for me to brag about my boyfriend Bernard. I told him how perfect Bernard was for the part he was looking to cast and how gospel was his forte. Well, Bernard got the job. He is the lead gospel singer in the finale of the film singing *Believe It.*

TR: How did the relationship with Barnard go?

TT: Things did not work out between us and we went our separate ways. Unfortunately, we had a mutual friend who had hidden motives. He misguided us and we separated. I do consider Bernard my lost love.

TR: Did you speak to Herbie Hancock after starring in his video?

TT: A few months after the video release Herbie invited me to join him at the first annual MTV Awards. That was in 1984. It was a real treat for me. I never experienced anything like it. Madonna performed her song *Like a Virgin*, and she rocked the house. It was scandalous. The coolest part was that she sat in the seat in front of me. I thought this girl has guts. She is a performer who is very powerful live.

TR: Did this inspire your move to Hollywood?

TT: By the end of 1986, I found a new love; a dancer named Angel. At the same time, the bright lights of Hollywood were calling me. Angel was originally from L.A so it took some talking to get him to move home. Nevertheless, I was successful and we headed for the land of make-believe.

TR: Did you have an agent in California?

TT: My first agent was Nina Blanchard. Professionally, L.A was a good fit for me and my dance talents were a plus! Videos were on the rise big time. Angel proved to be a big help to me professionally. He introduced me to many people.

TR: Did your agent get you booked on jobs?

TT: Yes, one of the first big jobs Nina booked me on was a Billy Dee Williams eyewear campaign. It was exciting to think that I was about to work with Diana Ross' leading man from the film *Mahogany*. To my surprise, Billy Dee arrived to the studio a bit liquored up. It was only 10:00 a.m. and we could all smell the alcohol on him. He was frustrated and preoccupied with a personal problem, mumbling on about something. Still, I was excited about this day and working with him. When we got to work, the mood in the studio was fun and light. I did get a surprise, though. The photographer positioned us with Billy Dee seated and me standing behind hovered over his right shoulder. The shot was a tight frame. Out of nowhere, his hand grabbed my lower private parts. I am certain that a shocked expression flashed across my face as I let a little scream out and jumped back. We did finish the shoot and the photographer called out the traditional ending, "That's a wrap."

TR: How did you feel about Billy Dee after that?

TT: I lost respect and admiration for Billie Dee that day. He hurt and disappointed me with his behavior. For a moment, I considered telling my agent Nina about it, but honestly, I did not want to cause a scandal or problem. I felt it was better to let it go and to forget it.

Besides, who was going to believe me? I doubt that anyone would have believed me over him. He was a big star and I was just starting my career and scandal was not what I wanted. I wrote it off as an invasion of privacy, but if this was a flirtatious gesture, it went too far. Excessively way too far!

TR: You mentioned dancing earlier, did you pursue dancing again?

TT: Yes, and Angel introduced me to his agents at Joseph Helfond & Rix. Because of my background in dance, he thought the pairing was good for the both of us because one of their agents had a department specializing in dancers and choreographers. Julie, who became my agent, was fresh and new. I wanted to remain with Nina as well but I could not be signed with both, so my decision would be JHR as they represented clients across-the-board.

TR: How was your relationship with Angel then?

TT: Within five to six months, Angel scored a dance gig with Madonna on her *Who's That Girl* tour. We had been through a lot in our relationship. I had endured and put up with more than I should have. I had problems in the past with him cheating on me, and I started to question his loyalty and infidelity again, because of rumors. Unfortunately, the rumors turned out to be true. The woman he was cheating on me with confronted me once. It was a hurtful and devastating experience. It was time for me to move on from all the pain. There was no loyalty on his part and the trust was gone. There had been others before her but she was the proverbial straw that broke the camel's back. I started to focus more on my career and my life. I concentrated on the issues that mattered to me. I felt a new sense of independence and power; a freedom, if you will.

Chapter Two
The Beginning Of A Dream

TR: With a re-focus on your career, what was a typical audition day like for you?

TT: In August of 1987, I was pounding the pavements by foot and the help of the RTD; the L.A. bus system. Coming from a New York outlook, I didn't think of a car as a necessity. Looking back, I have wondered how I managed without a car. However, I did figure it out and I worked it down to a science. First, I had to allow an hour for travel, sometimes two. If my destination was far, I'd always dress down and casual and carry my change of clothing with me. This way, if the audition required that I wear a dress and heels, which was typical, I was prepared. I did not think it was wise to dress to the 9's on public transport. It brought too much attention to me.

Once I started working steadily, I often spoiled myself and just called a cab. I loved being chauffeured. That goes back to when I was a child. I was very young when I left home on a ballet scholarship, so I never had the opportunity to learn to drive. At home, until the time I was thirteen my mother drove me to ballet classes. I saw the back seat as a haven; it gave me the freedom to stretch a bit; to warm up or change in the backseat. Most of all I loved the freedom of watching life pass by my window.

TR: What audition do you specifically remember? Which part did you want the most?

TT: It was the week of August 12 and my agent phoned to tell me about an audition for an artist but she was not allowed to reveal his or her name to me. Julie told me, "This is a big artist! It is a celebrity with the status of Prince or Michael Jackson." I remember wondering who it could be but then I thought, Oh well, It doesn't matter. A job is a job. Just be yourself and do your best. That is all you can do.

I lived in Hollywood and the audition was in Hollywood. The LA bus system was not going to see me that day. I decided to walk all the way. For a New Yorker, walking a couple of miles is nothing — nothing but good exercise. What a beautiful and sunny day it was. To this day, I find it incredibility ironic what happened to me a couple of blocks away from the audition. A group of construction men were hanging out on the street and started whistling at me. Now coming from New York, this seemed like typical street behavior. Like most New York ladies, I was accustomed to handling myself and not reacting. My belief is that the more energy you invest in something the more energy you have to put into finding an exit and a way out. I shrugged my shoulders and rolled my eyes, like yeah right, whatever! I was able to ignore and escape their presence by casually walking past them.

When I arrived, Leland, the casting director, went through the video routine with me. I could not help but laugh, since the story he described was exactly what I had experienced a few blocks up the street. I even half jokingly asked, "Why don't we go and get the guys to run through this?" I ran through the routine alone with Leland following me with a handy cam, and I put myself back in that 'on the street' frame of mind. It was perfect timing, with just having gone through those emotions; it proved to be a great warm up. As I ran through the routine a few times, I could not help but notice the music playing in the background. It was Michael Jackson's song *Beat It.* It was then that I knew in my heart, that it had to be for him. I mean really! It would be an insult to play Michael's music if the audition was for Prince. Artists are too temperamental and sensitive to do something like that. Once I finished my routine, it was off to the bathroom to change back into my street clothes; jeans and high-tops. My nerves were working overtime my adrenaline was racing. I was wondering if I had done everything to the best of my ability.

When I returned home, I let it all go. In this business, it is not worth dwelling over an audition or a reading. Once it's done, it's done. I knew that within my heart, I had done my best. By the following day, it was out of my thoughts. There were other auditions and more pavements to pound.

TR: Were you working on other projects at the time?

TT: During that time, I was booked for a Chevrolet commercial with seven other dancers. This was a mess of a production. The stylist changed my wardrobe seven times and the director did not know where to put me. Should I be in the middle? At the end? Leave it to me, that's my luck. Here I was again sticking out like a sore thumb. In the final edit, they cut my part out completely. Oh well! That's showbiz. I shot the Chevy commercial on the 18th and if I had had any indication of what the following week was going to bring, it would not have consumed my mind in the least.

TR: Okay, so what happened?

TT: August 29 was a day I will always remember for years and

years to come. Julie, my agent, was good at keeping quiet about this particular job because she had to. She never let on to me about the follow-up audition or callback until the day before. So when she called on Aug 28th, she reminded me of an audition I'd had nearly two weeks before. I blanked for a minute but, once she said, "The one you went on for the mysterious artist," it clicked! I said, "Oh, yeah!" She then admitted it was for Michael Jackson but, really, how could she not at that point? I knew from the music the day of the audition. I remember being so excited and a huge scream came out of my mouth! This was my first and only impulse and I never considered my neighbors or the effect it would have on Julie over the phone. However, Julie was as emotionally ecstatic as I was. We both spoke of the shock and excitement we felt. It was a secret between us for a while as I was clearly instructed not to say anything to anyone!

TR: Did you keep it a secret?

TT: Later that day, as I drove along La Brea and Sunset Boulevard with my friend, Audra Ribeiro, and a friend of hers—our music blasted loudly from the radio as we rocked in our seats, swaying to the music. A song came on that we had not heard before. A new one of Michael

Jackson titled *The Way You Make Me Feel.* I then became attentive wondering, Could this be it? Is this the song? Could the girl he is singing about be my part? Could I be the lead? As we kept our rhythm, we agreed that this song was a hit. I was just dying to tell her that I had gotten a call back for this very song that day. Once we got back to my apartment and I got Audra alone, I told her about the exciting audition I was looking forward to the next day. I never told her what artist it was for though. She swears she knew who it was saying, "It is Michael Jackson's nature to be secretive as an artist." I never did tell though.

TR: Were you nervous the night before the callback?

TT: That night it was so hard to fall sleep. I had problems with insomnia as a kid. I am just more of a night person than a day person. So, that night, I slept very little wondering what tomorrow would be like. Would he be there? What would he look like? Will I meet him? My God, what will I wear? Will I get to dance with him? Will he like my moves? Will he like me? On and on and on, my mind raced. I could not believe this was not a dream. This was really happening to me. I think I had a never-ending prayer to Jesus that night, because I never did fall asleep.

TR: It is now the morning of your callback. What happened?

TT: When that Saturday morning of August 29th, 1987 came, I was ready. I prepared my travel ahead of time; so much so that I was half an hour early. I was the first and the only one there. Michael was close to two hours late. Did I care? Well, it did not help my nerves at all. I was a nervous wreck inside. For the first time in my life, I experienced wet palms. I can remember reciting the melody of "Nervous is why you need Soft and Dry," from the T.V commercial. Ha! I swear I did! Eventually, more and more people started showing up, and then I felt a little more at ease. I realized that they were just as nervous and excited as I was. I then decided to get up and walk around to shake off my nervousness. I ran into actor Joe Senecca in a long hallway filled with artists' signatures on the wall. They asked me to sign the wall later that day. I had admired Joe Senecca's work since the movie *Crossroads*. It starred actor Ralph Macchio. I was feeling very intimidated by the events of the day but Joe was such a kind soul, and he gave me advice on standing strong and focused about my beliefs of my performance. He wanted me to feel confident and relaxed. I went in there with the attitude that I was going to knock 'em dead, and I can tell you with confidence that I did. I will always love Joe for the kindness in his heart and the gifts that he gave me, may he Rest in Peace.

As we sat around in a group, dancers and actors combined, a door opened. A guy came in and singled me out, telling me to follow him. This is what I had been nervously expecting, my cue. I got up and walked towards the door. I couldn't help but wonder if Michael was in the room. I walked through the doorway and saw a group of people sitting to my left. I wanted to turn and see if he was there but someone was directing me to come forward towards the front of the stage. It was Vince Patterson, the choreographer. Once I was on my mark, my concentration was intact. I looked out into the director Joe Pytka. I listened closely to his directions, as well as listening to the advice of the choreographer, who ran through the routine with me.

By the third run-through, I finally took a sneak and I saw him. It was such a quick glance that he was a blur. What stood out more was the color of his shirt. He wore red, a serious red! That excited me even more. I wanted to make a lasting impression when they brought in some actors for me to run through the routine with. I kept my eyes and focus on the floor while waiting. They positioned us and directed us on what to do. I held my composure as well as my cool. There were three other girls and about five guys. We went through the same routine a few times. They asked the others to leave, keeping me behind only to go through the routine again. I found out later that Vince suggested that Michael do a run-through with me, but he declined out of shyness. Therefore, Vince and I went through the routine a couple of times.

During the end of my last run-through, I looked out to see a smiling Michael. He was moving to the rhythm of the beat with a huge smile on his face. As I watched, I saw him turn to the person sitting next to him and point at me, and say, "She's the one." The entire time he had a huge smile, even a grin on his face. The joy he showed on his face made my heart feel light and as joyful as his smile. I later found out that what was in my heart was his remark.

His exact quote that came back to me was, "The rest are extras, she's the one- she's the one!" This remark came to me from David Banks, the writer who worked on the video. What a character he was!

I finished the routine and everyone was applauding, and for all I knew Michael might have started it. I started taking bows to be a bit comical with it, like a Lucy or something. Lucille Ball is my favorite, by the way. One of my best friends Eric Tyrus used to call me Luciana. Anyway, I walked out and I heard Joe Pytka say, "Don't call us, we'll call you." I replied, "Well, make sure you don't lose my number." I was dying to take one more peak at Michael, but I chickened out. What I did not realize until later that day was that this was Michael's 31st birthday, and what I thought was a callback was more of a rehearsal day. This was an opportunity for Michael to see his choices of actors. He wanted to see how we blended. The day lasted close to six and a half-hours, and they did pay me for it. I floated out of there and I never felt my feet. I could still tell no one of this day and what I had experienced. I was dying to tell Audra, one of my closest friends, or even Valerie Simpson who was not only my closest confident, she was also the manager of my building. However, I was required to sign a privacy agreement before the audition and I was not exactly going to let the cat out of the bag. Besides, until this point I was holding up well with this big secret. I could make it through another day or two to know the outcome. I wanted to wait until I knew if this was a done deal or not before I spoke about it. I floated all the way back home.

TR: So you did not tell anyone about the callback?

TT: I must be honest by confessing that the one person I did tell was my mother. I figured she was the one person even Michael would understand me telling. I rambled on and on about what it was like seeing Michael — especially that big grin on his face and how he had pointed at me. I was so excited that she could not get a word in edgewise. Anyway, she lived in Florida. Who was she going to tell? Okay, so she told my Dad!

Later that day, Audra came by to visit me and she admitted that she had driven by the audition site, on La Brea Avenue, to see if she could find out who the artist was. Of course, she could not, because they had trailer trucks surrounding the entire building, so you couldn't even see the entrance. Nevertheless, she kept insisting, "I know it's Michael! Who else is so careful about keeping projects so secretive?" I never said a word though. What a weekend that was. Better than eating a chocolate cake and to me, that is heaven on earth. My appetite suffered though. Who could eat with all this excitement? I have never been one who has put much time or thought into food. I have always been a small eater.

I always say, "I don't live to eat, I eat to live." However, that weekend I hardly even did that. When Monday rolled around, I was eagerly awaiting some news.

Chapter Three
Dreams Can Come True

TR: I feel like I was there with you that Monday morning. Did you get the part?

TT: Monday, the 31st of August, the phone rang and it was Julie. She gave me the dates that we would start shooting. I really thought that I was going to explode and die! Julie was telling me to block the dates from September 4 through 7 and things just went into a blur. I thought, Could this be happening to me? When Julie added, "You are going to be the lead girl," I could not believe it! I think I left my body.

TR: Did you get any sleep the night before the project started?

TT: The night before, sleep was impossible. I tossed and turned so much that I had to get up and walk around at times. I had so many thoughts and questions that consumed my mind and I never did get to sleep. Once the alarm went off, I jumped out of bed as though it was on fire. It did not take me any time to dress that morning because I picked my outfit out the night before. I was ready to see what this day had in-store for me.

TR: How did you get to the location? Did you actually take the bus as you usually did?

TT: The location was not close to my apartment and I wondered how I was going to manage to get there on time, especially at 7:00 am which was a fairly early call time. The shoot was in San Pedro which is quite a distance from Hollywood. This was an "A class" production and the expense for my transportation must have been peanuts for a Michael Jackson project. They had me chauffeured to and from the location by limousine every day. I thought this Hollywood stuff is great! My driver was such a gentleman and we had great conversation everyday.

TR: So you get to the location. What happens first?

TT: Of course most of us arrived before Michael. I reported in with the crew, hair, and make up artists. They asked all of us to wait in the trailers we shared. La Toya, Michael's sister, had her own and I did not mind sharing a trailer though because all the girls were great! It was about a month or so later that my agent admitted that she should have negotiated a separate trailer for me. It never even entered my mind, who could think on such a level when you are working with someone like Michael. I had been in L.A for less than a year. However, I will admit, it would have been nice to have had my own trailer if only because it was a bit crowded and I wanted to be focused on my work.

We sat around with shattered nerves waiting for Michael to arrive. Finally, they called us to report to the set and what an awesome set it was. I felt as if I was back home on the streets of New York City. It wasn't the Lincoln Center area where I had lived and studied ballet but it was familiar to me and resembled the feel of the city. There were streetlights and graffiti on the walls of the set and even a little New York style convenience store. Geoffrey Kirkland, famous for his incredible set designs built the set. It was four city square blocks and they completed it in ten days. It included a car and a stairway that led up the front entrance of an apartment building where I walked at the end of the video. I was amazed at how life-like the set was. It was breathtaking and we stood there taking it all in.

TR: Had you seen Michael yet?

TT: The time had come when a slim Michael came walking out through an alley. This particular alley is the one that I run down in the video that is a "dead end." I stood trying to control myself and keep my cool. I could not look directly at him, but I could feel his presence within the group of people that surrounded him. His manager, Frank Dileo, was to his left, and his photographer, Sam Emerson, was to his right. Michael stopped and stood about five feet away from me. I just could not believe the artist I most admired and loved stood just before me. It was more than a professional moment; he was the one for whom I secretly held a big crush. I just could not bring myself to look up at him! Instead, I focused on Vince Patterson who stood to my left.

Vince greeted Michael and they shared a few words. I didn't know for a fact but sensed that the two had a rapport. Vince turned to me and introduced me to Michael. He said, "Michael, this is Tatiana. And Tatiana this is Michael." Michael extended his hand to me, and I extended mine. I looked into his eyes and managed a quick and nervous smile. For some reason, I could not look into his eyes longer than a split second or two. His stare was so intense. His eyes were piercing right through my soul. Michael's presence was more powerful than words could ever express. I have so many memories of this time — some I cherish, and some that are so hurtful when I think back. Some are so painful that it depresses me to remember. I choose not to reflect on that part of my past very often.

TR: I understand. Tell me more about the details of the video shoot.

TT: The stylist and the director had me go through the wardrobe. Although we had agreed on the look the previous day, we tested other looks just to make sure we were satisfied with the wardrobe. We agreed on the black dress. It was the exact look that I put together myself for the original audition taping with Leeland. There was only one difference in my dress and their dress. Danskin made mine and theirs was an expensive Azzedind Alaie that was priced at around $1,000. The boots were mine, and the bracelets were too. I created my own look for the video and I was proud of that creative control, and that Michael liked what he saw. The only thing that they added was something that I had not considered. It was a track of hair weaves to add more length to my own hair. They told me that was Michael's idea.

TR: What was Michael planning to wear?

TT: I remember asking him, "What are you going to wear?" He replied, in a sweet and a soft voice, "This is what I'm wearing." I felt so embarrassed because I appeared to be very overdressed compared to his costume. I thought, how silly, I am dressed up like a working girl and here he is dressed casually. I did not get it and I felt that someone needed to change. Since I liked my outfit, it should be him. However, when I was around Michael, I soon forgot about costumes, hair, or make-up. I did not care. I was in bliss. I assumed that this boy genius knew what was right. After all, he had that video Midas touch. Once we started the routine I felt a little bit more at ease, but the whole time I still felt as if I was dreaming. The day progressed and I flew higher and higher into the clouds.

The Look for "The Way You Make Me Feel" Video

TR: How did the video routine play out?

TT: In the beginning of the routine, Vince went over the scene with me saying, "Now Michael is going to sing live and when he sings this part you are to walk in this direction." I agreed and I knew my cue, but when the time came, no such luck. I went into shock. Michael is very powerful live. All I could think of was that he is so small and thin so where the hell does that voice come from? How did he do that? As I stood in shock wondering all of this, Vince was screaming his head off at me, saying, "Tatiana, Go! React, Go, Go, Now!" Finally, something snapped and I woke up. I thought, oh yeah, I have something to do, too. I have to perform as well. I had a look on my face that reminded me of that Pepsi commercial. It is the commercial with little Alfonzo Ribeiro. It came out around 1986 or 1987. In the commercial Alfonzo turns around and finds Michael standing behind him. He is full of shock, surprise, and his mouth drops open. After the initial shock, I was able to get on with my character. Then Michael yelled, "Hey," to get my attention. Then he starts singing "You knock me off my feet, now baby." I start walking off ignoring him, but then a gang that did not let me pass through stops me. Michael follows me from behind, continuing in his pursuit.

TR: What happened at the end of your first day on the set? Did you talk to Michael before you left?

TT: Before going home he said, "Drive safe." I told him that I do not drive, I do not know how to. Someone drove me here. He said, "Tell the driver to be safe." I said, "Okay, I'll tell him."

TR: What did you do when you got home?

TT: When I got home, I was so wired mentally that sleep was so far from my mind. For those four days, sleep and food were not a big part of my agenda. I was running on excitement and adrenaline.

My normal weight of one hundred and one pounds was down to only ninety-eight pounds. Not such a big difference, but on my small frame a few pounds does make a difference. I looked forward to the next day as I had the first.

TR: Were you less nervous then you were the first day?

TT: Unfortunately, by the next morning my nerves had not improved any. I got up, dressed myself, did my hair and make-up and I was off to the set. I could not wait to see Michael again. I never wanted this job to end.

TR: What did you and Michael talk about the second day of shooting? Did you talk to the rest of the cast?

TT: With both of us being extremely shy, we did not talk much at first. We did smile and stare at each other many times though. The whole crew was great and the writer, David Banks, was wonderful. It was a primo gig. It was the gig of "all gigs." Even the real gang members that he hired were pleasant. I guess being on a M.J. set can bring out the kindness in almost anyone. The one person that I became close to on the set was Michael's stand in, Craige Parks.

We sat and talked about how awesome the set was and how wild it was – being such an amazing replica of New York. We also talked about how the guys were real gang members. I told him how excited I was to work with my idol. Craig had worked with Michael several times before. He told me about his experiences with Michael and how he loved practical jokes.

The last days of the shoot with Michael, for me, had gotten better. Everyone became more relaxed and natural. That is when Michael and I shared a special moment, the Icebreaker. This was the same morning that Joe, the director, treated me a way that I would have never expected. He took me by total surprise.

TR: What did the director do that surprised you?

TT: I reported to the set. I stood across from Joe waiting for his direction as he yelled at one of the grips. I remember thinking, my God, this is how he treats his people? That is terrible. I had no idea that mine was coming soon. As I started my routine, he snapped! I do not even know what I did to receive such treatment, not even to this day. He started yelling, "You stupid, fucking bitch! What's your fucking problem? Didn't you have your fucking coffee yet?" My eyes got big, my ears grew red, and my heart became pained. I could not believe that he was treating me like this. I stood frozen in my footsteps. I felt tears welling up in my eyes and I was choked up with so many emotions that I could not even swallow. I felt I couldn't control the tears that were about to flow from my eyes. I heard him say, "Let me know when you are ready to work." I became determined not to let his negative aura get the best of me. I replied, "No, let me know when you're ready to work," and I ran off the set. I ran into the dressing room and I cried for about five minutes. I poured out all the pain his words caused. A few of the guys and the stylists asked me what was wrong, and why I was crying. My emotions took over so I could not reply. I just could not speak at all. I was balling my eyes and heart out to the extreme. Joe Pytka is known for this behavior, and I was slowly learning this. Someone told me that he had a lawsuit against him because of it. He was physically abusive towards a grip. It was amazing to me that he treated me this way, and I could not believe that he worked with such negative energy. I mean, people noted him to be the best at his craft. Cindy Crawford had admitted to his temperamental personality when she made her Pepsi Cola commercial years ago. She said he called models names like "BIM and Bo." She admitted to him calling others girls names, but never her. Of course he did not dare try to do this to Cindy Crawford. She was too famous!

TR: Did you go back to the set?

TT: Yes and when I reported on the set I was willing to forget about it. Just for the sake of professionalism, but I will never forget it. It was surprising that Joe's attitude changed suddenly once I returned. He was a bit kinder.

TR: Why do you think he changed his attitude? Do you think he realized what he did?

TT: I later learned that Michael's photographer, Sam Emerson, watched him yell at me and went back to Michael to report it. Frank Dileo, Michael's manager, was the one who spoke to Joe. Whatever he said, it helped. Joe never openly attacked me again.

There were little comments like, "You're not a star! Tatiana Petitze, the model is a star." Tatiana Petitze was a famous supermodel at that time. He whispered that in my ear. I thought this must be his way of making me stay humble or something. I just could not figure out the mind-set of his treatment. I do feel that I can honestly say, I am and have remained humble throughout all the Hollywood weirdness. I feel that I am as real as they come. After all, I am only a human being.

TR: Did Michael say anything to you about what had happened?

TT: By this time, Michael arrived on the set and seemed concerned about me. I could see it in his eyes. He even brought it up. He asked, "Are you okay?" I expressed that I did not understand why Joe used that language. It was not so much him yelling at me as much as the language and tone he used. I told Michael that I was a lady and I did not expect treatment like that from anyone. We soon forgot about it. I was just happy that Michael had arrived. A bit later La Toya, Michael's sister, and mother Katherine arrived. I wanted to meet them. The thought of meeting more Jacksons was exciting. I remember thinking how close La Toya and I were in size. She disagreed and said that I was even smaller. I did not learn until a year later that we both shared the same middle name, Yvonne.

We talked a bit and I discovered that our favorite vegetable was broccoli as we waited to shoot our group shots. I met Michael's mother at lunchtime.

TR: How did you meet his mother?

TT: There I was standing near the end of the buffet line waiting for it to move. I saw Mrs. Jackson at a distance with a friend, Janet Simms, who later became my hairdresser. They started walking towards me. I remember thinking Oh My God! She is coming towards me. Michael's mother is coming towards me. What do I say? I just could not help but be star struck by her. As she stood next to me, I only mustered up a shy smile. Janet introduced us. She said, "Mrs. Jackson this is the girl Michael's working with, Tatiana." I said, "Hi, nice to meet you." Then she went to look at the buffet to see what it offered, but she never walked away with anything. To be honest, I could not help but think that she was checking me out. She wanted to see the girl she had heard about. The girl that had captivated Michael's interest or tweaked Michael's curiosity, and I eventually found I was correct about her suspicion. She admitted it to me later.

TR: Michael talked about you to his mother?

TT: Yes, and later in the day, there was an incident that has become a fond memory. We were shooting the scenes in which I run from Michael by going through this beat-up car, and he follows me. It was the second take and by that time, I was having much fun with the scene. I made faces at him in the car and then ran out leaving him stunned. By our fourth take, the heel of my boot was caught in the cars upholstery and Michael put his hand on my leg to help pull it out. It blew my mind that he had actually touched my leg, which I pulled away and began to tumble out of the car falling on my butt and hard too! Michael started laughing hysterically as Joe Pytka yelled, "Get up, keep it going, keep it going, and don't stop." As I did, Michael got out of the car and started wiping my butt off.

I could not believe it! Michael was flirting with me. I thought if anyone had ever questioned his manhood, here was his or her answer. This was a guy who didn't care about expressing his likeness or attraction to me in front of others. It broke the ice of our shyness between each other and it gave me a rush. We laughed about that one for a while.

That fall caused a run in my stockings and the stylist wanted me to change. I started walking off the set and Michael asked, "Where are you going?" I explained that she wanted me to change my stockings. He disapproved by saying, "No I like it. I think the run is neat. It is sexy." I found that comment was a masculine statement, and personally, I did not think the run would matter.

Who would care if I had a run? On the other hand, who would even spot it in the video? No one ever did. However, that one moment was the most memorable of the shoot, except for the final scene when we hug. It made me realize that dream's can come true. Michael also told me that he loved my walk and said that it was very sexy. This I felt for sure was a compliment from a heterosexual male.

TR: Did the two of you continue talking?

TT: Between a break, I admitted to him that I saw him years ago in New York walking ahead of me and that I followed him for a few blocks. It was during the time when he was filming the movie, *The Wiz*. He said, "Oh really? Why didn't you say something? You should have said something." I replied, "Because I was too shy and couldn't think of what to say." This was truly ironic; I had followed him several years before on the streets of New York and now here he was chasing me in his video.

TR: What happened the rest of the day on the set?

TT: As we continued shooting the car scene, I was choreographed to run towards my girls, while we laughed and made gestures at them; making fun of Michael and the 'guys. I then walked off, like "yeah right," and walked around to another car; a Volkswagen where Michael started a game of hide-and-seek. Next I walked up to a street bench and sat down while he tried to get my attention. I tried not to focus on the fact that we were coming close towards the end of the video and I kept trying not to think about it.

TR: How were you feeling that night knowing that the following day would be the last day of the shoot and maybe the last day you would see Michael?

TT: That night, as I was lying in bed, it was very sad for me. All I could think about was that tomorrow would be my last. I fell asleep with much sadness in my heart. The morning sun came and I awoke with excitement of seeing Michael's face again.

TR: So how did the last day go?

TT: We began with a scene in which I run up to an apartment building, avoiding him again, and then I run back down the stairs. Michael told me, "Whatever you do, don't fall down the stairs or I'll start cracking up." I was thinking what a brat. During a quick break from this scene, Michael pointed out two birds high above us perched on a ledge — they were making love. He said, "Look," while pointing up. I became embarrassed and shy and I looked away blushing. Michael stood gazing at me with this sweet smirk on his face that was somehow very naughty.

TR: What was it like watching Michael dance live and up close?

TT: Watching Michael dance with his group was one of the most beautiful sights I have ever experienced. My dance experience gave me a deep level of appreciation for the opportunity to have been a part of all this. I had already seen some of the greatest acclaimed dancers ever — Rudolph Nureyev, Mikhail Baryshnikov, and Edward Villella. Michael was a perfectionist. I admired how he emulated the mood of the legendary work *Westside Story* but in his original and completely fresh version. I didn't realize it then but I was falling for him. My heart was growing and my emotions were becoming wrapped up in him.

TR: What are your other memories?

TT: Michael had some interesting and exciting guests visit the set.

I met Corey Feldman, Emanuel Lewis, and Kadada Jones; Quincy Jones' daughter. When we were introduced, she was not friendly to me at all and the only thing I could not figure was that she would have disapproved of any girl Michael chose for his video.

TR: What happened as you approached the last scene?

TT: Michael had requested a closed set for the final scene in which we hugged, No one was allowed other than people necessary to the shoot. No dancers, visitors, or extras. It was quietly rumored that we were supposed to kiss at the end of the video scene but Joe came up to me and whispered in my ear, "Don't kiss him, he's too shy for that, don't kiss him!" Therefore, of course I respected his direction. I would never question an order from the director. As I stood and turned to my right, I looked out to see Michael. He approached me we stared deeply into one another's eyes. I felt as though he could see my sadness and could hear my heart. He placed his arms around me and mine around him. I remember him stroking my back up and down as to say, "I care for you too." You can see this in the video. I felt it was all happening much too quickly.

The weirdest thing about that scene was the way the light hits the water. It actually made the shape of a heart behind us. Between the scenes, Michael said to me, "I heard you wanted to dance in this video." I admitted it was true and I said, "I thought I would get the opportunity to dance with you." Michael replied in a soft and sweet voice, "Don't worry, we'll work together again." Suddenly I felt content and confident that his words were true, and my heart felt light with joy. As I began to put deeper thought into it, I realized, he had not answered the question about why I had not danced in the video. My dream had been to do a Fred Astair and Ginger Rogers number; dancing as equal partners. However, it did not linger in my mind for long after his promise. I settled for what I got. I mean, how many people even get that close to a dream? I was fortunate, in starring side by side with him. It was the Fred and Ginger of the 80's as far as videos are concerned. I was thankful to Jesus a million times over, and I knew then that dreams do come true. I have lived a few and I hope many more to come.

TR: Did anyone on the set notice there was something going on between the two of you?

TT: One of the actors said to me, "You like him don't you? I can tell you both like each other. I'll bet you'll end up getting married and have ten kids." I remember thinking, ...with my little body I don't think so! One of Michael's own security guards even asked me during a break if I had a boyfriend. He asked as if he was asking for Michael. Michael stood by doing some out takes and I waited around and watched with my new buddy, Craig.

TR: How did you feel at the end of the day?

TT: When his final shot came, I was sad and a bit depressed knowing the end was near, as we walked Michael off to his trailer. He thanked me for being so professional and I remember being a bit surprised. Those were golden words to my ears as I expressed how great it had been working with him and then he asked me if his team had my number. I floated out of the trailer. As I left, I could hear Michael say to Frank, "Aren't you going to give it to her?" Frank replied, "No, why don't you give it to her? It's from you." They were bickering like kids and before I knew it, Frank tossed one of Michael's hats to me. A black fedora with his name embroidered in gold inside the rim that he used in his *Bad Tour*. I caught the hat as if on cue and as I walked off, I recall saying; "I love you, Michael." I guess the fan was coming out of me. Or maybe I could just not admit that my comment was much more personal. I did not own one Michael Jackson album or tape at that time so my feelings were based on respect for him as an artist and what I came to know of him as a person rather than being a fan. Of course, I owned the *Bad* LP when we finished the project. I was honored to have been a part of the history and the making of the video.

Several days later, I finally got my appetite and my sleep back on schedule but working with Michael had been one of the greatest natural highs that I had ever experienced.

TR: Did you keep in touch with anyone from the project after the video shoot?

TT: I kept in touch with a few of the cast members like David Banks, who was one of the writers, and Craig, Michael's stand-in. David warmly called Michael, "Junior" and he called me, "Peewee." He constantly teased me about my size! He said, "You need to go and check out Fredericks of

Hollywood and get some help. You could use what they've got." He was referring to the famous Hollywood lingerie store known for making 'padding' fashionable and it made me laugh so hard. David mostly wrote comedy skits for shows like Sanford and Son. He kept me in stitches; he was one nutty character.

TR: What was next for you? Was there other work coming up?

TT: Two weeks later I auditioned for another video; this was for the legendary group The Temptations. I didn't meet with them prior to the shoot as I had done with Michael, but I met with their director.

TR: Did you get the part?

TT: Yes, we shot on Thursday, October 1 but there were no luxuries like a limousine, and the set was not as elaborate. My co-star was Billie Dee Williams who I had worked with a year earlier. I had mixed feelings about working with him again, but I found some comfort in the fact that there were more people around us this time.

TR: What were the Temptations like?

TT: Meeting the Temptations was exciting. During the shoot, I had the pleasure of working with Fred "ReRun" Berry from the television show *What's Happening*. He was a gentleman, and Bill Tannan the director was a real pleasure. I wanted to like Joe Pytka, but after he had chewed my head off with such evilness and vulgarity it was kind a hard.

TR: What was your wardrobe like for this video?

TT: Once again, I was able to bring my on style into play. My dress was designed for me by a young French designer and a friend of mine named Deni' Mazouzi. This was an exciting time in my career and I had no indication it was all about to change.

TR: What was the location for the video?

TT: We shot the video in Santa Monica at the male 'strip-club' Chippendales. There was a big earthquake in L.A. that day. Big enough to shake the boots off the entire set of male crewmembers. They all ran out and left me inside when it happened. They left the make-up artist and the stylist behind as well. I guess it was every man for himself!

The Temptations manager, Shelly Burger, expressed an interest in representing me. He was also Billie Dee Williams manager and at one time managed the Diva herself, Miss Diana Ross.

TR: Did you do any publicity for either of the videos?

TT: November was my first introduction to Hollywood publicity.

My first interview was for Entertainment Tonight, the crème de la crème of entertainment television. I was also booked to do an interview for *PM Magazine* for *The Way You Make Me Feel* video. It was all exciting, but I was nervous about doing the interviews. I asked my agent, Julie, to attempt to find out the questions beforehand so I would not have any surprises, so that I could be prepared. However, I learned that it does not always work that way. At that time, Julie was acting as my manager, my agent, my publicist and my confidant. We made many mistakes together as I was one of her first clients to be the focus of such hype. She was fresh and too green as an agent, and I eventually paid a price for her lack of knowledge. Another of her clients whose career did grow was Paula Abdul who I had worked with as a dancer in a commercial.

On December 30th 1987, I had an interview with *People Magazine.* Todd Golden did the interview by telephone. I was pleased with the interview. That was my first experience in realizing that things do not always show up in print in exactly the way you say them in interviews. Just the same, I was proud of the piece and Julie was ecstatic. She asked me; "So how does it feel to be on the same page as Cher and Elizabeth Taylor?"

After *People Magazine,* I was set up by Michael's team to do interviews for the music channels, BET, VH1 and MTV.

On January 5th 1988, I met with Willie Harper, the director of the interviews. We hit it off right away and he was a cool guy. We had a meeting before the job to go over all of our ideas. I was so happy because he was the first and only director who gave me so much creative input and it was awesome being a part of that. We did a ten-hour day and my ex-boyfriend Angel was hired as choreographer for the dance sequences. While Angel and I were not able to work out our relationship, I still believed in his talents as a choreographer.

Tatiana didn't kiss, and won't tell on, Michael Jackson.

On January 18, Martin Luther King Day, I was scheduled for an interview on *Hour Magazine*. Gary Collins and Vicky Lawrence were the co-hosts. I was very nervous about this interview because it was my first experience; live and in front of a studio audience. When I walked onto the set, Gary immediately began talking about my debut in Michael's video and asked about the excitement that I might have been feeling. They were showing the footage from *The Way You Make Me Feel* video and at the same time they were asking their questions. Vicky Lawrence commented "Boy, those dance lessons didn't pay off at all." While it was true, that I did not get to show my dance ability in the video but it was obvious to the eye that I am a dancer. You can never deny a dancers' stance or walk. It is something that is always with you. After the videotape ran its course, Gary continued asking me questions and Vicky commented, "I'm going for the juice kids. Let's get the gossip." She intervened with remarks like, "She looks like him." Gary replied, "No she does not." Then Vicky said, "She looks like Diana Ross?" Again, Gary insisted "No, not at all." I finally could not resist and said, "No Vicky, I'm one of a kind." That left the audience humming oooooh's and aaaaah's, as if to say, I had gotten in a good one.

Julie received a letter of apology from the talent coordinator of the show and in the end it was a good lesson for me on how to handle myself in front of the public and on a live television show. Nevertheless, it turned me off and I was no longer a fan of the TV show *Momma's Family* that Vicky Lawrence starred in.

TR: Was Vicky asking her questions based on some of the rumors that were going around about you?

TT: Yes, many rumors were flying. One of the funniest was that I was one of the Jacksons. They said that I was a cousin that no one had seen before. I remember cracking up hysterically about that one.

Back home, one of my Dad's friends, Bob Henderson, was a newspaper reporter for the *Tampa Tribune*. Bob did several stories about me and I was proud that my hometown gave me positive attention. That wasn't the first time I had been in our hometown paper. It was reported when I received a scholarship from *The School of American Ballet* and when I received the key to the city of Clearwater. I credit my ballet teacher Beatriz De Paris, and the Gulf Coast Ballet Company who honored me with an Alumni Salute in 1989.

TR: Did people begin calling you for jobs?

TT: It got very busy. Doors were opened but sometimes appointments were scheduled just to be stared at. I was called to meet at the game show *The Price is Right*. They admitted that they just wanted to see what I looked like in person and wanted to meet me. They even asked me to sign autographs for their kids. You can just imagine the disappointment and how it felt like such a waste of time. On another interview, the casting director asked me why I had not worn the dress from *The Way You Make Me Feel* video and asked where the dress was. I said to him "She's at the cleaners."

TR: Were people starting to recognize when you were out in public?

TT: When I went about my normal life; running errands and such,

I came to the realization that something had changed. I was suddenly recognizable. I was a face people saw twenty-four hours a day on all the music channels and it was all new and rather strange for me. It was exciting yet, scary. On one occasion someone followed me home. That was scary! I had experienced a taste of fame six to seven years earlier as a model working in Japan but this was now on an entirely different level. It was worldwide and people from all parts of the world stopped me to ask for an autograph or picture. I met people from France, Germany, Africa, and Italy just to name a few.

TR: Did you see or talk to Michael after you shot the video with him?

Receiving the "Key to the City" of Clearwater

TT: In January, Michael was shooting a new video entitled *Leave me Alone.* His stand in, Craig, was working with him and to my utter surprise, he called to say that Michael invited me to come and visit him but that I would need to clear my visit with Michael's personal secretary Joli. I was ecstatic at the thought of seeing Michael again. My heart raced with the warmest and happiest of feelings. The location was in Culver City and I only had forty dollars with me which I knew wasn't enough to get there and back but I figured I would worry about that later. I just could not pass up the opportunity to see Michael again especially since he had invited me.

TR: Did you think it was odd that you would have to get your own clearance from Michael's secretary?

TT: From what I had learned, Michael had everything done for him. Craig was adamant that I had an invitation from Michael but who knows, maybe it was a way in which to impress me a little bit. He had given me the phone number of Michael's personnel secretary and that was a big deal.

TR: Were you excited to see him again?

TT: When I arrived, I was so nervous and excited to see him. I remember taking a big breath as I pulled open the big studio door.

To my left, Michael stood on a small platform that was about four to five feet off the ground. He wore a yellow, Hawaiian print shirt with a ball and chain wrapped around his leg. It was the funniest site. I had arrived between takes and Michael seemed genuinely pleased to see me. For the rest of my visit he was full of smiles. Craig and I hung out while Michael did his scenes and for a short break.

Sam Emerson, Michael's photographer, asked that Michael and I pair up and do some photos. He took a full roll of film and they gave me two of the Polaroid's as a gift. In one of the shots, Michael was cuddling me and in another, I was wearing his long black coat. He told me that *The Way You Make Me Feel* single had charted number one that day and Michael complimented the earrings I was wearing. They were of a little boy and girl engaged in a kiss. As we finished the photos, Michael's manager Frank Dileo arrived. Michael joined him in his trailer and a few minutes later they asked me to join them. When I stepped into the trailer Dileo took control, as Michael seemed to be a little uncomfortable and at a loss for words. He kindly asked me to have a seat and join them for some pie. Michael sat next to the window and I sat beside him as Dileo took the containers out of the bag. Michael impatiently, like a kid, opened his up and started to chow down. Frank asked, "So, how is it going?" I started telling them about my interview for *Hour Magazine.* Michael was inquisitive and seemed to know nothing about it. Frank, on the other hand, was aware of the interview and began explaining the scenario to Michael. Frank then offered me some of his banana cream pie which I later learned is one of Michael's favorites. When I dove in to get a piece, somehow I ended up with a larger slice than Frank's and I jokingly remarked that I needed more of it than he did anyway. Frank was taken back by my comment and his face turned red. It did not help any that Michael was cracking up about it. Although there was some truth to the comment because Frank was a bit of a hefty guy, I truly meant it in a humorous and innocent way. After a few minutes of small chitchat, Frank told me that he and Michael needed to discuss business.

TR: Did you think Frank's statement was to dismiss you because of your comment?

TT: I wished I had not made the remark but I had not said it with any bad intent. MJ just kept laughing like a kid. In fact, Frank laughed it off as well. Nevertheless, I do not think he said he had to discuss business because of my comment. They left soon after. Frank was always rushing off somewhere. It was not long after that Frank approached me about representing me so I don't think he was offended by my pie remark.

TR: What happened next?

TT: I returned to the studio to hang out with Craig while Michael continued his shots, Craig and I stood nearby with Michael's make up artist Karen Faye. Michael and Craig were laughing about something between them, like a private joke as I stood next to Karen. She asked me what was going on — why they were laughing? I replied that I did not know, and I didn't. I was simply smiling from the joy of being there. I was on cloud nine. I could feel Karen's negative energy – probably because she felt I was holding something back from her. The rumor floating around was that Karen had feelings for Michael so it made complete sense that she despised me and she did not try to hide it. You can feel a person's heart when you look into their eyes. Anyone could tell that Michael and I had chemistry when we were together. It was obvious to the eye and there was talk of his feelings about me going around. Craig was constantly telling me that Michael was asking about me and Michael would ask him to relay hellos to me.

TR: Did you and Michael talk more that day?

TT: Michael commented on my jacket, telling me that he liked it. It was an orange color bandleader's jacket. It was very Michael Jackson indeed. Later, in 1989, I sold the jacket to the celebrity re-sale shop *A Star is Worn,* in Los Angeles.

Before I knew it, I heard the final words, "That's a wrap!" I told Michael's assistant Miko Brando, Marlon Brando's son, that I did not have a way home and asked if he would mind giving me a ride. He told me that he was sure it would not be a problem but for me to mention it to Michael and to see if it was all right with him that I ride with them. As Michael approached me to say good-bye, I asked if it was okay with him that Miko was going to drop me off. His eyes lit up big with surprise but he sweetly said, "Sure no problem."

TR: What was the ride home with Michael like?

TT: As I stepped into his big black Mercedes, it amazed me! It had everything - a T.V, a VCR, and a phone. I wanted to tell him that he was driving my all-time favorite car but I did not dare because I felt that if I did, I was taking the chance of sounding like a gold digger or being too materialistic. However, it was a beautiful automobile! I felt like royalty sitting in this beautiful and roomy car with the world's greatest artist and icon.

Miko asked me for directions to my house while Michael sat nervously. He looked as if he did not know what to do with himself. He was cute. We talked about our families and he asked if I had any sisters and brothers. He shared with me that he liked being part of a big family.

We stopped at a light on La Brea Avenue and there was this cute little black girl standing there with her mother. She had braided hair with little colorful bows all over. Michael said, "Look how cute she looks. Her mother did her hair in cute little bows." All I could think of was, if this little kid only knew who was in this car talking about her it would probably make her day. I considered asking Michael to roll down his window but they were already crossing the street.

Once we got into Hollywood, we passed the famous *Hollywood Roosevelt Hotel.* From my window, I pointed it out to Michael, and I told him that I had worked there as a hostess before doing the video with him. Michael asked, "Hostess? What's that?"

Miko intervened and explained what a hostess was and Michael cut him off by saying, "OH! Yeah! Yeah! I know."

I asked Michael why he always wore tape wrapped around his fingers tips during his performances. He explained that the tape gives an elusion of extension for dramatics. I thought how ingenius, and I told him, "You are a genius!" Michael loved this compliment as he smiled from ear to ear. He said sweetly, "Oh thank you." I placed my hand on top of one of his hands and then I picked it up and put it in both my hands holding it gently. I could feel his nervousness. Then suddenly he picked up the phone as a call came in from his secretary Joli. I let go of his other hand so he could manage the phone. He remarked that my hand has a roughness to it like his sister's or members in his family. He didn't say this in a bad or insulting way and it's true. My hands are of an old soul, and other people had noticed this before. I felt that Michael liked me touching him but that somehow he just did not know how to deal with it. He acted very shy about it.

As his Mercedes was pulling up to my door on Orchid Avenue, just up the street from Grauman's Chinese Theater, I thanked him for being so kind and for driving me home. I also thanked Miko. Michael told me that he wanted to wait and watch to make sure that I got inside my building safely. I thought that was so sweet but I could not help but think, please God, don't let me trip. Whatever you do, do not trip. I can be the biggest klutz, especially when I am nervous or excited.

As I made it into my doorway with out any blunders, I turned around and saw the Mercedes slowly pulling away. I reminded myself of how lucky I was to have the world's greatest artist driving me home. I felt like Cinderella. To think of all the childhood dreams I had about meeting Michael, and here I had worked with him. I was even chauffeured home with him, his driver, and his friend. I boasted about this day to my mother. I told her everything about that day and how wonderful Michael was.

I knew that I would be the envy of many, and I was so thankful for my blessings a million times over. I was falling more than I even realized for him. You could not speak ill of Michael in my presence, or I would chew your head off. I found myself defending his manhood when others put it in question.

TR: Did you try to contact Michael after that?

TT: The following month I sent Michael a valentine card. I wanted it to be special so I enclosed one of the earrings that he said he liked; the one with the little boy and girl engaged in a kiss. I thought for sure that would make my card stand out from the norm. I wanted it to have a romantic overtone. I contacted Joli for this mission.

TR: Were you working at this time?

TT: I had a neighbor named Tony who was an actor, and he was preparing for a role in a film entitled *The Perfect Model.* Through Tony I learned the director had an interest in me for a part in this film. I got the part and I found out later that I was replacing the singer/actress Vanity. She was Prince's girlfriend for a time and was once a friend of mine. The film was shot in Chicago, "the windy city." I had a cameo appearance with only one day of shooting.

The American Music Awards were on January 25th, the same evening that I was supposed to fly to Chicago so I flew on a red-eye after the awards show.

On February 8th, Frank Dileo, requested we meet at his office in Ventura. I remember being very excited until I got there and realized that Michael was not there and he was not going to be there. Frank told me that he had been Michael's manager for a while, and confided that his luck could change any day. Michael could move on and get new representation so he had to think about future prospects and other clients. He expressed that he wanted to represent me. He told me he could tell

I had a thing for Michael and advised me to move on from my affections for him. He told me to focus on my career instead. He confused me. I did not understand his comments or his advice. He said that Michael and I would still be working together, and he gave me a tour jacket as a gift but he never came right out and told me that I would be a part of the *Bad Tour*. Somehow, I just did not trust Frank. I guess because he was telling me something that I just did not want to hear, as far as me moving on with my affections for Michael. He also made a comment about having me come over and see his new home someday, but without mention of Michael being around or his own family being there.

We then discussed the request I had received from Michael's office to audition for his upcoming *Dirty Diana* video and he disagreed with the idea of me doing another video for Michael. He said, "You don't want to be known for doing too many videos, and the role is a negative character. Just leave it be."

I left his office analyzing every word and comment. I didn't understand or agree with his advice of not doing another video with Michael. After all, I was an actress and a variety of roles; even with the same artist could be an opportunity to grow as an artist myself. I was trying to read between lines that I did not understand. I remember thinking that I didn't completely trust him, but then I was beginning to grow distrustful of almost everyone in Hollywood.

The following week on February 17, I got the incredible news that I had been added to the *Bad Tour*. The words that Michael uttered so sweetly to me while doing the video, "Don't worry we'll work together again" rang clear. Now I understood Frank's reasons for giving me the tour jacket. I was determined to think that Michael had feelings for me too and this was his way of telling me. My agent, Julie, fueled my thoughts when she told me she had heard that Michael had a thing for me. Before I knew it, the tabloids jumped on the story.

THROUGH
STREET

Chapter Four
A Taste Of Touring

TR: What were you thinking the first day that you arrived to start the *Bad Tour*?

TT: I joined the tour in Kansas City on February 22, 1988. When I arrived, I met up with Miko. After picking up our luggage, we were off to the hotel. The hotel hospitality from the management and clerks was as if I were royalty. They personally escorted me to my room and to the bellman's horror; we walked into a room that had not been made up yet. He apologized profusely acting as if a crime had been committed and he told me that he would return after reporting this to his manager.

I dropped my bags off in the lobby where I saw Karen Faye and her assistant Anne Morgan. I chatted with them until the bellman returned, reporting that management was honored to have me as a guest, that he was moving me to another floor and insisting that management wanted to express their regret for an unmade bed. He gave me a key that provided elevator access to a floor that had a beautiful corridor and led me directly to the door of my suite They had moved me to a private floor and one of the most beautiful rooms in the hotel. It was just awesome! I could not believe it.

When the management told me that they were honored in having me as a guest, the truth was, I was honored in being their guest. Most of all, I was impressed with their hospitality. Unfortunately, When we returned to L.A, I heard from someone that Karen Faye started a rumor that I complained about the service at the hotel and that I had demanded a suite. I was stunned, to say the least, but I knew that Karen did not like me. I could sense it whenever I was near her.

I had twenty minutes to enjoy this incredible room before heading off to the stadium. When I arrived at Kemper Arena, I met up with my director and my friend, Willie Harper. They assigned him to do the piece I was scheduled to do for *PM Magazine*. The original concept was for me to report on the tour but they changed the story line, using me as the focus of the piece. I hated this idea. I wanted the opportunity to show another side of me. I wanted people to know that I was not just some Barbie Doll; to prove that I could walk and talk, too. Willie shared my frustration.

The entire time we were doing some of the outtakes, someone from Michael's team tagged along. Willie and I did not like the odd feeling that we were being controlled or watched. After a few takes, I was scheduled for a quick run-through with Michael and the band. So much was going on and everything was so moving so quickly. I never got a chance to thank Michael for including me in the tour. Every moment was so rushed and I felt as though I was in a spin cycle.

The rehearsal took about half an hour and then we went back to *The Marriott Plaza*. The band and crewmembers were in one hotel, while Michael and Frank were in a completely different hotel altogether.

It was finally showtime and I was more excited than words could ever express. I was sitting in the make-up chair when I heard the roar of the audience responding to Michael. It was my cue, and I found myself being very nervous. I was counting down while one of the roadies escorted me down a long hallway towards the stage entrance. I knew my cue, but for some reason I still questioned myself. This was the most wonderful experience ever! I heard people actually yelling my name, and I could not believe it. Some were saying; "Hey, It's the girl from the video!" Even that was wonderful to hear.

TR: What were you supposed to do onstage?

TT: Michael and I emulated the characters and choreography from *The Way You Make Me Feel* video and it went over very well in the live setting.

TR: What happened when the song was over?

TT: PM Magazine was there with cameras when I came offstage. They asked, "What does it feel like being a part of the show?" Suddenly, my heart was saddened that my parents were not there to be a part of this experience. I managed just to say, "I'm so happy," but I was choked up with emotion. I hate going back and thinking about this because it still makes me very emotional.

After the *PM Magazine* questions, I started balling my heart and my eyes out. I used Miko's shoulder for the next five minutes. He kept me company and he kept an eye on me. That seemed to be part of Miko's job because he was always there.

That night I joined up was the final show in Kansas City; followed by five days off. I spent most of my time in my room watching movies and I was bored. The only person that was socializing with me was Miko.

TR: Why was he the only person you socialized with?

TT: I came to learn, through one of the band members, that Michael told them to stay away from me and not to bother me. I thought this was respectful of him to do and my mother especially liked it!

TR: Why do you think he told them to stay away from you?

TT: The way I perceived it, then, was he being protective. Michael knew that men could be "dogs" and the tour scenario just invited trouble. On tour, he wanted them to know that I was his personal interest.

TR: What were some of the things that you and Miko did together on your days off?

TT: On one of our days off, I offered to baby-sit Miko's child, because it was his birthday. At one point, I saw Miko autographing photos for Michael. I found it odd and I thought it was very dishonest — especially when a fan was paying so much for a ticket. I did not question Miko about it, though. I just figured that maybe this was normal for someone of his stature. Miko's copy was almost identical to Michael's, at least to the naked eye it was.

TR: So where was your next shows location?

TT: On the 29th, we were off to New York City — the city of dreams and my home away from home. I could not help but remember the creative visualization I had done leaving New York for L.A. The words that ran through my head were, "Someday New York, I'll be back in style." I guess you could say that creative visualization does exist and I am a strong believer in it. With that, and a good amount of willpower, you can accomplish anything in life. I remember sitting on the steps of my building on 54th street years before, depressed and crying because I did not have a ticket for the Victory Tour and I felt as though all of New York was going except me. Here it was four years later and I was on tour with Michael Jackson. Now that was irony!

On March 1st, the PM Magazine piece aired. To my surprise, but not to my dismay, the story read as though Michael had found his soul mate in me. On this day, I left a message with Michael's secretary Joli, and I told her that I wanted to speak to him. She explained how busy he was, but she said that she would give my message to him.

TR: You mean PM Magazine reported that you were Michael's soul mate?

TT: Yes! The piece was about us working together and it was reported as though he found his love and his soul mate for life. They meant with me.

TR: When and where was your next performance?

TT: The following day, March 2nd, we performed for the 1988 *Grammy Awards* at the famed *Radio City Music Hall.* Now I really felt on top of the world. This was history in the making. When we ran through the rehearsal, I was so happy to see Michael again since it had been six days since the last time that I had seen him.

TR: Did the two of you get to spend any time alone together?

TT: At one point, as I was powdering my face, I realized that he was watching me. Before I blushed or even had a chance to get embarrassed, he asked if he could use some. I could not believe he was asking me this, but I was honored to share it with him and we were going onstage so it was a natural thing. I watched him use it and it was a sight to see. He was going to town with the stuff. I almost cracked up about it, but of course, I did not for fear that he would take offense. I treasured that compact with sweet memories. Unfortunately, a so-called friend of mine stole it from me. It really hurt me to think that she would do something like that to me. This was someone I knew for years and someone that I trusted. That was my memory to share, not hers. People can be so cruel and cold hearted.

TR: So what happened during the rehearsal?

TT: Our routine was going to be different for this special performance. Michael started by singing, *The Way You Make Me Feel*, and then he went into *The Man in the Mirror*, combining the two songs.

During a short break, Quincy Jones played a practical joke on Michael. He placed a photo of Prince on the seat next to him. Michael nodded his head as to say, "No Way!"

While the rehearsal continued, I had some off time so I sat in Michael's seat watching. I caught Mike smiling at me with approval and a gleam in his eye.

After a couple of hours, it was back to our hotel, *The Parker Meridian*. I couldn't resist in calling my parents and keeping them informed on the day's events. It was sad to me that they were not there to share this joyful time in my life, but I kept thinking they would join me in another city.

TR: How did it feel to depart for a performance at *Radio City Music Hall*?

TT: We piled into the tour bus, and as they escorted us to the entrance and to my complete surprise, fans were yelling my name. I could not believe it! One of the dancers even made a comment saying, "Oh, so they know your name now huh?" This comment was sarcastic and made me feel a little uneasy. All I could think of was how weird this all was. Four years earlier, I had cried about not being able to attend a Michael Jackson concert, and now here I was a special feature in one. I was overwhelmed with my blessings. It was wild! Limos and celebrities were everywhere.

As we gathered in one room waiting for our cue, I heard Michael through the door of a private room going through his vocal warm up. I noted how powerful his voice was! One of his security guys remarked to Michael that I looked beautiful and I heard Michael reply, "I know." He did not even see me yet.

Before I knew it, the incredible Stevie Wonder and his entourage were escorted inside. Yes, I was in awe.

TR: Did you get a chance to meet Stevie Wonder?

TT: Yes, someone introduced us and when he asked for something from the buffet, I was more than happy to hand him an apple. When I did, I told him how much I admired his music, and I told him that he was "BAD," which really meant good in 80's slang. Stevie laughed and told me, "No, this apple is BAD. That is what's bad because you gave it to me. You are BAD."

TR: What an event even before show time!

TT: It was! Finally, we were escorted through the many hallways and the stairs of the music hall that lead to the stage. As we took our positions, the audience went silent in anticipation of us coming onstage.

Peaking out from a curtain, I saw the faces lost in Michael's magic. They were in a trance. I suddenly heard the familiar beat and the signal for my cue. When I stepped out onto the stage I passed Mike and heard him say, "Work it! Work it! That's it!" A comment like that inspired me even more.

We had decided during rehearsal that I was going to catch his black fedora hat but ultimately the idea was nixed. Instead, I walked off the stage and I blew him a kiss.

TR: What happened off stage?

TT: I stood in the wings watching the rest of Michael's performance. I was deeply lost in a trance like everyone else. Someone walked in front of me and as I shifted my position the woman turned to me and said, "Oh! Excuse me!" It was the one and only Miss Diana Ross. She was the woman that Michael admired as he grew up. Well, so had I.

TR: Did you talk to Diana?

TT: Yes. I even shared with her that people told me many, many times, that I looked like her. She had this expression of surprise on her face and had no comment what so ever. Then, we both stood watching Michael's performance and I focused on the monitor set up nearby. I sang every lyric and Herb Albert who was standing near me said, "I see you know every word, don't you?" I smiled and continued to sing.

TR: What happened when Michael finished his performance?

TT: They rushed Michael backstage. He stood nearly five feet away from me covered in a black cape with a white towel around his neck. There were many people around him talking to him and I didn't dare

get near him. I did not even try. I just watched from where I stood. I did yell, "You were great Michael!" At first, I did not think he heard me but he did a few moments later say, "Oh! Thank you," in his soft Jackson voice. I was thrilled that he acknowledged me and before I knew it, he was whisked away like Zoro.

TR: Did you watch the rest of the show?

TT: I watched with some of the dancers. I was enthralled with seeing my second live music show – the first being the Herbie Hancock appearance following the video we had done.

TR: What did you do the day after?

TT: The next day on the 3rd, it was off to *Madison Square Garden.*

This was our first tour date in New York City and still I had not had the opportunity to speak with Michael. I wanted a one-on-one with him. I wanted to thank him personally for making me a part of his tour. There were such brief verbal exchanges during our rehearsals and somehow, I just did not think it was too much to ask for.

TR: So, you had not spoken with him yet?

TT: The only time I saw Michael was onstage, or on television. I was usually alone in my room watching movies or wondering what Michael was doing. Being on tour can be a bit boring especially if the other members had been told to stay away from you. Honestly, this rule lead me to believe that Michael was going to spend some of his down time with me. I mean... Why not? Everyone was passing all these little mentions and comments from him to me. I often asked Miko about him, and asked what he was doing?

It had been a week and I was still waiting for a response from Joli. I figured it could not hurt to try her again. She told me to be real patient and that he was really busy.

On the 4th, we had down time and I once again spent part of my day off in my room with Miko.

On the 5th, I wrote in my diary that I was depressed and wanted to go back to L.A. I was receiving regular phone calls from a reporter asking me all sorts of questions about Michael and me. I put him off by saying, "I gotta go" and quickly hanging up. He would call right back and eventually I relented when he asked, "What's it like working with Michael?"

I finally gave in and replied, "I love It, It's great!" Well, that was my first TABLOID experience. What was printed was that I said, "I love him." It was true of course but I would never, ever, have said such a thing. After his call, I was out the door to get ready for the show.

While Karen Faye was doing my make-up before the show, I found myself trying to make small talk. I had a feeling that she did not want to talk — she had such a bad vibe with me. I asked her, "Do you really think there is a resemblance between Michael and me? People are always saying we look a bit alike. Even the *PM Magazine* piece compared us calling us, "Soul mate look a likes." She replied bitterly saying, "Oh! Not at all! You two look nothing alike." Her tone was of such disgust and negativity that I did not say another word. I let the conversation go, stood up to go the bathroom and pushed onto a swinging door. Well, as I was pushing in, someone was pushing out. To my shock and pleasant surprise it was Michael's little sister Janet.

TR: Did you talk to Janet?

TT: I asked her to take a quick snapshot with me and I told her that I thought she was a good dancer. She gave me a "NO," reply like the one Miss Ross had given. She just starred at me with these big eyes.

TR: What happened next?

TT: As my cue grew near, my nerves began working overtime. I was escorted down a long hallway towards the stage entrance. I ran into Madonna and she was making her way, to leave, I think.

We shared a few quick words and as I entered the back of the stage. I once again found myself questioning my cue.

My boot hit the stage and the roar of the audience greeted me. It was massive! Leave it to the New Yorkers to let you know how they feel. I walked out in character making fun of Michael and his homeboys while making hand gestures at him; basically, making fun of them. Strutting back and forth across the stage, I stopped, grabbed his collar and said, "Come on Mr. Big Shot." I was calling his bluff, changing up the routine a bit. As I grabbed his collar, I landed a big wet one on his cheek. I kissed him. I did not think anything of it, and I did not think that he would be ticked off. I just thought it would add some excitement to our performance.

A Magazine photograph, reporting that I was "Michael's Girl"

TR: What was the response?

TT: The fans went berserk! They loved it. After I left the stage, I heard a laugh in every note Michael sang. I figured from his laughter that he enjoyed the surprise. The dancers told me that he was happy and excited by the kiss. Telling me,"OOHHH, Boy! You made Michael's day! He was happy!" I pretty much thought it was a good thing.

TR: Was that the end of it?

TT: In the dressing room, I wanted to take off my make-up, but there were celebrities everywhere! One of the reporters teamed me up in a photo with the very tall Brooke Shields. I saw La Toya, Michael's sister, from a distance and I decided to join her. We stood talking, and someone from the press asked us to pose for a photo which was later published in *Rolling Stone*. That magazine photo was one of the coolest experiences in my life.

After taking the photo, Frank came over to me and said, "Good show kid," while patting me on the back. Meanwhile, I was overwhelmed by the entire thing. There were so many stars waiting backstage. They were all hoping to see Michael. I doubted that most of them would get to see him , because he usually did his Zoro act and disappeared. I never saw him after a show.

TR: Did you finally get a response?

TT: The following day was our day off. Once again, Miko was entertaining me. We had lunch, and yes, I asked him about Michael. Walking home from lunch, I saw my old friend Vanity on the cover of *Playboy* magazine. Suddenly, Miko and I were in a heated discussion about whether or not I would consider appearing in *Playboy*. Miko argued that I would and I argued that I would not. He insisted that I would do it for the right price.

Later that night we took another walk. I told Miko that I wished I could take a horse and carriage ride with Michael. He asked me if I were crazy. He said, "Mike could never do that! He would be recognized." I argued with him that he would not. I mentioned how he could disguise himself, as he is known to do. In my mind, Miko was losing this argument.

March 5th we had another great show. Afterwards, *CBS* threw a party in Michael's honor. I remember seeing one of my favorite actors, Christopher Walken from a distance and being star struck. Joli, Micheal's secretary, joined me. She told me that she knew Michael had feelings for me, because he spoke of me often. Yet, she stated that she was confused about why he had not responded to my request to speak with him yet. She promised me that she would make the call happen. I was fed up with everyone telling me that Michael liked me. Everyone but the man himself was telling me that he liked me. I did not get it. It just was not making any sense to me. Or course, it felt odd that I could not even speak to the guy that supposedly liked me. Still I was thankful for the wonderful experience that I was having, and I remained hopeful.

That following morning, I woke to the realization that this was my last date in New York. John Draper, the tour coordinator, told me that they wanted me to rejoin the tour in Atlanta. I was ecstatic and I wanted to see and thank Michael more than ever now.

TR: Were your hopes fulfilled?

TT: Preparing for the show, I stepped out of what was my final luxury bath in my suite at the *Parker Meridian.* The phone rang and it was Joli who jumped right in to say that Michael was really tired and not feeling well so to keep the conversation short and brief.

Joli said, "When you call him ask for Bill Bray. He is Michael's personal assistant and he will put you on with him." I was ecstatic! I was so excited my hands were shaking and my heart was beating so loud I swear I could hear it. I paced for about a minute and then I decided to just get it over with and call him or I might chicken out altogether.

As I dialed his number, I felt like I had the worlds winning lotto digits. When I called him, Michael answered the phone, not Bill Bray. It was as if Michael had been expecting my call. I asked him how he was doing and he answered; "Oh fine, I'm just a little tired." I told him to take it easy and to take care of himself. I brought up our last show together. I apologized to him because I had kissed him on the cheek. I said, "I am sorry if I threw you off in anyway," Mike intervened by saying, "OH! No! No! It was fine! It was great! I liked it." Then I asked him, "Well, would it be all right then if I did it again, and perhaps take it a step further?" He said "Oh sure! That'll be great!" After all, he would sometimes pull a girl out of the audience and embrace her. Why would a kiss from someone you like be a big deal? I explained to him that fans were always asking, "Why does Michael chase you through this entire video only for a hug?" I then said to Michael, "Well, thank you so much for inviting me to be a part of the shows. It has been so exciting. I love being out there with you. It is a blast."

As I got dressed and made-up that night, I was excited about my conversation with Michael and the secret I felt we shared.

When I stepped onstage, there was that roar from the audience again, they were fired up. They truly liked me too, I thought. When I approached Michael, my heart was fluttering. For a few brief seconds, I thought about whether or not I should follow through on this kiss. For some reason I was questioning myself. As I stepped up to him and put my arms around his collar, he looked deep into my eyes, almost as though he was challenging me. Then he did this sexy little thing where he bit his bottom lip. I placed my arm around his waist, and I landed a kiss right on his smacker!

Never for a moment did I feel this was one-sided, as he at this point, put his left hand on my rear. Anyone witnessing this historical event saw that this was a mutual effort. I nearly fell off the stage because of the adrenaline rush in my body.

TR: How did everyone respond to your kiss? I mean, at this point no one had ever seen Michael kissing a girl in public. This had to be shocking to everyone.

TT: I walked towards the dressing room and down the hallway afterwards and I ran into Frank Dileo. He had this expression of hard disappointment on his face. His eyes said to me, you have done it now. It was an evil look. Until this day, I bare a scar on my soul from this look, and from the entire experience. He did not say one word to me, and in the past he always said, "Great show kid," and gave me a pat on the back.

I stood frozen, knowing that something was wrong. Then I reminded myself about the conversation that we had, and that Michael agreed to the kiss.

The next person to greet me was Michael's mother Katherine. She walked towards me and gave me a big bear hug. I was so touched by this and, for the moment, I forgot about Frank's cold evil stare. She actually hugged me. Katherine Jackson put both her arms around me and very warmly hugged me. This meant a lot to me. She later admitted to me that she saw absolutely nothing wrong with us kissing. She approved.

Later, the National Enquirer wrote that I was the first woman Michael ever kissed in public.

At the hotel after the show, John Draper, the tour coordinator, approached me about signing some forms for the bill and told me that I was to rejoin the tour later. I was standing with John and Miko came at me from no where. He was yelling at the top of his lungs. John and I stood frozen and in shock. Miko was in a rage. He yelled, "How dare you fucking take advantage of him like that! You fucking bitch! Who the fuck do you think you are? I cannot believe you fucking took advantage of him like that in front of all those people." He kept on and on, and I could hardly get a word in but finally I said as calmly as possible, "Michael and I spoke about it over the phone before the concert. He said it was okay." He eased up a bit. Then I said, "I would never take advantage of him. It takes two to tango you know!" I ran to the elevator, choking up and about to explode in tears. I had never, been so humiliated and embarrassed in my entire life. He showed no diplomacy or class by approaching me in the manner he did. I guess he yelled at me because he thought it was my fault. I could not believe the tabloids did not write about this incident. They love this stuff. Miko apologized to me later that night and asked me to give him a call before my flight that evening.

TR: What happened when you returned to Los Angeles?

TT: I returned on March 6th and that week I did a *French Vogue* spread.

Then on March 9th, I did a national commercial add for *Tre' LA* and an interview for *Ebony Magazine* on up-and-coming starlets. I admitted in the interview that while people treat me like a celebrity I did not consider myself one. I said, "I think that when you're a celebrity you have financial security." I was referring to the months that I still could not pay my bills on time. That year, I made the most money that I had ever made and I had not even made $40,000.

On March 18, I was scheduled to fly to San Francisco to work on an assignment with Willie Harper. It was an educational video teaching children to never smoke. I somehow got on the wrong flight and of all the strange events, I ran into Rebbie Jackson, Michael's oldest sister. Is that unbelievable? I just could not get over this odd coincidence. I had never met her and I found her to be very warm and charming. It was as if we had known each other for years.

After realizing that I was on the wrong flight and headed for a destination with no one to meet me, she insisted that I join her and her husband Nathaniel. I waited with them at their hotel, trying to reach Willie. There were moments that I was just dying to tell her that I was crazy about her brother. However, I did not for fear she would think I was fanatical. Nevertheless, it was the beginning of a new friendship.

Rebbie and I ran into each other during our travels another time too. It was many years later, and wildly enough, we were both in Japan.

At this point, I was also seriously considering representation for personal management. I was in negotiation with a female named Terri Hartman. Her mom was a respected producer and publicist and her sister is the famous actress Lisa Hartman. I figured my days with Frank Dileo were over and I liked the idea of having a women manage me. I did not feel it to be threatening at all. She booked me on a couple of talk shows.

On March 29, I was off to Cincinnati for an interview and it was a first-class experience. They even agreed to me bringing a friend. The driver picked us up in a triple stretch limo, and we were embarrassed because of its size. It was gaudy and I felt like it was screaming "Look at me!" People were trying to look inside and if you had seen this giant thing turn corners, it was a trip.

When we reached the hotel all the staff was a buzz, it was as though Michael, himself, was there. I got a few phone calls from fans that found out I was staying in the hotel. One pleaded and even cried to me asking me to forward a note he had written to Michael. I kept this promise and sent it to his office.

That evening we had a blast. My host took us to Club Coconuts which was one of the hottest club's. The owner of the club introduced me to the magician, David Copperfield. During the introduction, the clubs DJ played *The Way You Make Me Feel,* and I was embarrassed. David asked me to dance and before I knew it, we were entertaining the entire club.

The next morning I did an interview for two different shows and tried hard to keep up with all the bombardment of questions. After that, we were on an early flight headed back to La La Land. It was March 29, and Terri scheduled an interview for me to meet with an agent at the *William Morris Agency*. I was very excited about the possibility of signing as they are major agents in the industry. I felt that I had outgrown my agent Julie. As my agent, she overlooked too many things. Someone showed me a 45-single of *The Way You Make Me Feel* with my picture on it. After finding that out, I heard about a 1988 Michael Jackson Calendar. Again, my picture graced the month of May. I was not paid for the use of my picture and image. I asked Julie about it and she had no comment, questions, or professional advice on the matter.

TR: Wouldn't it be standard business to be paid for the use of your face to sell a product?

TT: Yes, and many, including my pal from the video shoot, David Banks felt I was being taken advantage of from all around. I'll never know the facts, but several professional people led me to believe that my own agent had not had my best interest at heart, and suggested that she might have taken more than her cut. He could not believe that I was paid a mere $5,000 for the tour and a little less than that for the video.

People were pointing out that I was excluded from some of the most typical things; for example I should have received a copy of the plaque from the song. *The Way You Make Me Feel* charted Platinum and as a part of the success everyone who had even the smallest bit to do with the video probably got one. I felt shunned to say the least.

TR: Did you get the chance to speak with Michael about this?

TT: Not a day would go by without a prayer to God that eventually I would get the chance to speak with Michael and clear up any misunderstandings. I do not know how or why I thought I could have this opportunity, especially after my tour experience. At this point, I tried desperately to keep my focus on work, and I struggled to remain positive.

On April 6, I had a hair appointment. I was horrified to find out that I had three bald patches on my scalp the size of half dollars. I was suffering from so much stress that I got Alopecia; a condition caused by trauma and stress. When my hairdresser found the bare spot's on my head, she practically screamed saying, "God, that tour had you stressed out, didn't it?" I freaked out. I did not know if my hair was ever going to grow back. I cried so much and so hard during this time in my life. It was almost too much for me to bear. My friend and confidant, Valerie Simpson, was my pillar of strength. She was the shoulder I leaned on.

Constantly, I asked myself why Frank Dileo had given me such an evil stare. And why had Miko screamed at me the way he did in front of everyone? It all pained me! Joe Pytka was probably somewhere saying, "I told you so."

TR: You were supposed to rejoin the tour, correct?

TT: I was nervously waiting to rejoin the tour and everyone kept asking me about it.

On April 11th, I appeared on *The Tonight Show* with host Ross Schaffer. Ross was the host before Jay Leno took over. He asked me, "So are you and Michael really dating?" I replied, "No, we're not. Our relationship is strictly professional." He insisted, "Oh come on!" I repeated my answer and once again, he insisted with the point that we were dating. I thought I would add a little humor and some mystery so I responded by saying, "No, we're not. Not yet anyway." It got back to me that Michael did not like my response. Supposedly, I was some plotting broad and I was up to no good. I could not believe it. I just could not win.

Two days later, the tour moved to Atlanta, Georgia. That is where I was to rejoin the tour. I was still expecting a call.

TR: Did you have any other work lined up in case they did not call you back to the tour?

TT: Yes, I flew to New Jersey and did some studio work in the hopes of getting a record deal. This helped keep my mind off things and it was a creative release for me. I knew one of the producers from my days of living in New York. This was a completely new process for me and I felt they expected a lot. If I hit the wrong note they would shut the lights off and make devil like voices. It was not very inspiring nor was it the experience I expected.

Someone else wrote the songs and I did not have any input about the material. I did not even like one of the songs that we were working on. The experience was not what I had hoped and the project crumbled like cake. They wanted me to sign an exclusive deal with them as my producers and my idea of a good deal included other producers as well. Producers that did not play devil like voices while I stood in the dark. Therefore, the possibilities were lost for what could have been a great record deal with *CBS*.

On the 21st, I worked with Mario Van Peebles on a film that he and his father had written entitled, *Identity Crisis*. Mario and I had known each other from our modeling days in New York. They gave me a cameo appearance in the film and I was happy I had the work.

The next day was my birthday and I celebrated it with one of the producers and Mario at one of the hot nightclubs at the time.

When I returned to LA, I received a call from John Draper. He wished me a happy birthday and then said, "I'm so sorry about what happened to you." I had no idea what he meant, so I asked "What do you mean what happened to me?" I sensed he was caught off guard. He continued saying that he thought that I was a sweet girl and wished me good luck. I still had no idea what he was trying to say to me. I started to worry and think about it everyday. I kept calling Frank Dileo, but he never returned my calls. I called MJJ productions, and they did not return my calls either.

TR: So you knew he basically was saying sorry to you because you were not going to rejoin the tour?

TT: Exactly, he was basically saying "sorry, you're fired" without fully coming out and saying it to me. He thought someone else had already told me. He thought that I knew.

The following week on the 25th, I did a two-day shoot for *Elle* Magazine. During my interview for the piece, the writer, who shall remain nameless, told me that a friend of his wanted to hire me for a clothing line campaign. He said that his friend had contacted MJJ productions to get in touch with me but was told that I was booked, unavailable, and in Europe. Well my friends, I have never been to Europe.

This not only devastated me, I felt as if a knife went through my heart. To think that my idol would do something so cruel was impossible to believe. Could he really be responsible? Would he do something that could damage my life and career forever? Could it have been people from his own camp? Was he aware of what they were doing? I pondered these thoughts for so many months. Of course, I wondered if I had lost other jobs or possible clients like the clothing line without even knowing it. What could I do? What had I done to deserve this? Yet, I could not ignore some of the rumors that floated my way. Someone told me they heard that I was being blackballed. That one really played with my mind.

TR: Do you really think someone was trying to blackball you? If so, who do you think was really behind it?

TT: I doubt I will ever know for sure if I was being blackballed but it sure looked like it and felt like it. My opportunities and job offers dried up quickly. Some obvious doors would not even crack open for me. My mere presence would sometimes reek of an odd vibe. I did not understand any of it. Once I became aware of the rumor, it made sense. I knew and felt something strange in the air. Who was blackballing me? I do not know and I certainly don't know why. I was unprofessionally fired from MJ's tour and basically kicked to the curb. Then, his office was telling clients inquiring about me that I was in Europe. I did not want to believe that someone from MJJ was to blame. In my heart of hearts, I never wanted to believe that. I could not believe that he was the one doing this. Until this day, it is hard for me to believe such a thing. That is why I welcome the idea of speaking to him. I want to find out what happened and why. I would love to have that opportunity, and to be able to find peace with it.

TR: Did your agent try to get you as much work as possible at the time?

TT: On May 25, I auditioned for a Seagram wine cooler commercial, which my friend Mario Van Peebles recommended me. The clients had concerns about my voice, because I am very petite and they assumed my voice would be light and airy, but I have a bit of a raspy, somewhat deep voice. Therefore, they scratched their idea of dubbing my voice and said I was perfect for the job.

Terri was keeping me busy as much as possible. I was doing photo shoots with great photographers like Gregg Gorman for Italian publications such as *Max* and *Stern* magazine. She even booked me as a judge for a *Miss Teen USA* Pageant.

August 26, was a very confusing and troubling day for me. I received two calls. One was from Craig, and the other was from the Jackson family. Craig started out by saying that he was concerned about what had happened – referring to John Drapers call. I thought for sure, I was going to find out what was floating around in the mysterious air. I asked him to explain. He carefully explained that Michael's back-up singer a young woman named Sheryl Crow, was replacing me in my part on tour. I was devastated by this news and I cried extremely hard after we hung up. I thought I was going to go crazy or die of this pain. I just could not believe it! I could not believe that Michael would hurt me by replacing me. I had created this character at my audition. Now someone else would play my part, in my dress! I could not believe what Craig had told me. I think I floated out of my body at some point to try to escape this horrific mental anguish. I went through a great battle with depression. I cried often and extremely hard. Then to top it off, I was bombarded with questions about why someone else was doing my part? People asked me, "Why aren't you out there? Why did Michael replace you with her?" All kinds of comments came my way, and it hurt so BAD. It hurt too much to be questioned about it as often as I was. It got to where I hated leaving my house. I felt as though I did not want to live.

My agent who had represented me for the tour had nothing constructive to offer about why I was not going back. I had been "added" to the tour, as a trial, and Julie had not required any type of contract. She made so many mistakes along this road. However, I did experience many more lessons in the land of Holly-weird.

Later that evening, the telephone rang again. This time I was really surprised. It was the matriarch of the Jackson family. Yes, Michael's mother called me saying she was very interested and concerned about me. I first spoke with Rebbie for a few minutes and she said that they were concerned about me. They wanted to know why I was fired from Michael's tour and she stated that her mother wanted to speak with me herself. This was the first time anyone had actually used the words "fired." Although I was told that I was being replaced, it still did not sound quiet as bad as "fired."

Mrs. Jackson got on the line and her voice was soft and sweet yet; it was filled with an enormous amount of concern and anger about the situation. She told me that she and the family were going to investigate some things with Michael's camp. She said there was something going on that they did not like. She asked me many questions. Questions that I could not answer. I told her that I did not know what was going on, and that no one ever told me that I was fired. She comforted me and reassured me that she was going to look into this and some other things. She invited me to her home in Encino. That very day, I sent a birthday card to Michael at his office.

The *MTV Awards* were on September 7th, and I was preparing for

Michael because he was nominated for an award but would not be present to accept it as he won as he was still on tour. An MTV producer had received the okay for me to accept an award on Michael's behalf if he won. I thought this was weird! I mean, they had just unprofessionally fired me and now he agreed for me to except an award on his behalf. Even though it was odd, I was absolutely thrilled.

Terri took me shopping for the event and bought me the most beautiful dress. I felt like Cinderella, and when that evening rolled around Michael did win the award. As I prepared to go onstage and accept for him, the announcer said, "Since he could not be here tonight, as he's still on tour, we accept this on his behalf." Well, so much for that! No one informed me of the change.

TR: Did anyone even give you some idea about why you were fired from the tour?

TT: On September 14th, I read an article in the *Globe* tabloid that disturbed me. It basically read; *"Michael ditched his traveling companion, a leggy, lovely Tatiana, because she talked about their friendship to a European publication. Silence, she learned too late, is golden where Michael is concerned."* I knew better than to believe what was written in a tabloid yet, it bothered me. Anything I ever said about Michael was good or positive. Michael was my hero and my idol, after all.

My friend Marie Gabriel, sent me another article from *SUN*, which is Britain's answer to the *National Enquirer.* The headline read; *"Love shock for Jacko sexy sizzler drives Michael wild."* The story itself read as though we were in love. Including photos from the famous or should I say, infamous, kiss they copied the *National Enquirer* story.

The quote that Michael gave to the press really blew me away. According to one report they quoted him saying; *Jackson stunned concert fans by locking himself into his first public kiss with Thumbzten. "I love her because she's warm, caring and exciting," Michael said.* This led me to believe that he was falling in love with me.

On the 9th, Michael was back in town and I spoke again with Mrs. Jackson on the 14th. She reassured and comforted me once again. She said that I would get an opportunity to speak with Mike and find out what the problem or confusion was. Michael's family felt this was Frank

Dileo's doing. It was clear; they did not trust his manager.

Michael's mother put me on the telephone with someone working with her and with her husband Joseph. He was a real character, named Jerome Howard. He told me that he was working with them and helping them with their investigation. He admitted to me that Michael's own parents could not get in touch with him when they wanted to and he was there to help find out why.

Jerome picked me up for my first visit to the compound. He took an interest in helping me with my career. My own parents felt some form of relief and hope from all the promises the Jackson's and Jerome Howard made. He talked a lot about the things I should be doing to capitalize on my success – like having my own clothing line, my own calendar, or my own doll. He told me how perfect my face was for a doll and the great success I could have. He promised it would all happen if I stuck with him.

My mother advised me to write Michael a letter during this time and to pass it on through my new contacts within the family. I was constantly in touch with Jerome. He called me, almost everyday. When I finally went to the Jackson family home, I could barely believe that I was there. I had seen photos of it in magazines like *Ebony* and *Life*, and now I was actually there! I was hanging out in the kitchen with Michael's mother and his sister Rebbie telling them how lonely I was when I was on tour and how I only saw Michael onstage. Then I told them how Frank and Miko had treated me after the kiss. I expressed everything I had endured and I told them some of the things that I thought were odd. Katherine listened to me with great interest. She said to me that she knew her son had real feelings for me because he told her so when we were making our video together. She said that one morning, before the shoot, she found Michael sitting on his bed. He looked troubled about something. She asked him what was wrong. Michael told her that he had real feelings for me and he wanted to know what he should do about it. Katharine said to him, "Just tell her, and let her know." She asked me if he had ever told me anything about this or his feelings for me. I told her no, but everyone told me that he had some feelings for me. It was clear to me that she was sad about the situation. She felt that Frank Dileo had something to do with it all. I brought up the fact that Michael had sent a request to my agency for me to audition for the *Dirty Diana* video, and that Frank had discouraged me from doing so. Her response was of more or less "Ah, ha, you see! You are a threat to him. If Michael falls in love and wants to marry you, then Dileo fears the person Michael is close to, could have more value and credibility than he does with Michael." She made a point I never considered myself. It was interesting that my parents and the Jackson family shared the same theory.

Katherine encouraged me to tour the grounds and she warned me to be careful of the swans out back telling me that if I got too close they would bite. I remember standing on a little bridge staring down at these swans as they glided in rhythm and wishing Michael was there with me. David Banks told me that I was living in a fantasy world, but I did not see it yet.

Terri kept me busy as possible with PR work. Unfortunately, it does not pay much if any.

Sinbad, the comedian, did help me land a role on the television show, *A Different World*. Working with the show's producer, Debbie Allen was a treat and a trip. She asked me one day, how big Michael's penis was! As if I knew, but I guess she thought I did. My answer was nervous laughter. I would never discuss such a thing anyway. To me, it would have been inappropriate. I am just too private a person for such personal talk.

After shooting the intro to "*A Different World,*" I learned that they did not want to use me as a regular on the show. Debbie promised me that she would bring me in as a guest appearance. That was part of her deal with Terri for me doing the show's intro. Instead, I was required to do a last minute audition. It was the worst of my career. This was a lesson to me in many ways, and I was reminded of Harry Belafonte's advice. He said, "Study your craft and be ready because they will throw you out and get rid of you if they can." Debbie's secretary admitted to me that she felt there was some kind of a conspiracy to keep me off the show. She told me to promise not to say anything or they could fire her for telling me this. She was telling me all of this, as she reached into a drawer and handed me a piece of fan mail. It made me wonder just how much mail really came in for me. I never exposed this information to Debbie when

I ran into her at a nightclub several months later. She told me that a producer was looking for me for a job but that she could not remember whom. This is what is known as a Hollywood mind game, and that is putting it in a nice way. Even some of the cast members stopped saying hello to me.

On October 21, I got a little black and white kitten. I named him, Magic Michael. He seemed to help me a lot, therapeutically, during those times, and he still does as he is here by my side.

TR: Did the problems get worse or better?

TT: On December 5th, I found out about the 1988 Michael Jackson calendar. One of my mother's students bought one and brought it to her attention. You would think I would have known about it and that maybe someone would have at least given me a complimentary copy. This was the second item with my likeness on it that we were aware of. I was very disturbed and bothered to say the least. For one, I was having financial problems and to think of all the countries that these items were being sold; the U.S, the Orient, the U.K and Europe. It made me sick to think that if I was paid just one penny for every copy sold, how comfortable I could be. I mean, I could have been financially secure for the rest of my life.

At the same time, I started seeing reports about a little boy named Jimmy who became a permanent fixture on Michael's tour. I recalled seeing him in the Pepsi commercial as well. I actually felt a twinge of jealousy toward this child. I could not understand why Michael chose to spend time with Jimmy and not me. There was even a report in the media that Michael took him and his family shopping. He bought the parents an expensive car and he took the boy on a spree to FAO Schwartz. The same student who brought the calendar to my mother's attention asked her innocently, if he had taken me shopping or bought me a car.

TR: Did you attempt to contact Michael again?

TT: On September 22, I prepared a letter for Michael. Katherine requested that I do so and I passed it on to Jerome, who was to make sure that it reached him. I never found out if it did.

There was another Jackson family friend named Majestic. He called me a lot and was the mediator between me and the family. He told me that at one time, he and Michael were close friends. He painted a picture of some of his experiences with the Pop Star.

He told me one of his many stories which was that during a video shoot, Michael, had him pull down a shade in his trailer. Michael told him, "If the fans see me do it, it will make me look bad to them."

Majestic was trying to shine some light on Michael in a kind way, showing me how Michael manipulated situations and people. The more I would hear of the family's complaints and stories about his own family not being able to reach him, it all made me think about who was really in control. I started questioning some of these things, and was bothered by so many issues. I did not like thinking negative thoughts about my idol.

TR: Did you date anyone at all during this time?

TT: I had a dinner date with the hilarious and talented Eddie Murphy. While on the telephone with him, I spilled my drink and said, "Oh, hold on I just spilled my Pepsi." Why I said Pepsi, I do not know because it was a Coke. I do not drink Pepsi. Eddie replied in that distinctive voice "OH, You are just all Michael Jackson-ed out." This was during Michael's big Pepsi campaign. In truth, he was right with his analogy, because I was crazy about him. Mike could do no wrong in my eyes.

During our conversation, Eddie explained that he normally went everywhere with his entourage, but that he was going to make an exception this time and come alone. It seemed a little funny and odd when he said, "Make sure your looking fine and dress nice," as though I was going to come dressed in a burlap sack.

When he arrived, I must say that it astounded me. He pulled up in a beautiful powder blue Rolls Royce. Eddie told me that Michael's own brother's disliked and were frustrated from seeing Michael's back-up singers do their old material. This was especially the sentiment shared by Jermaine, who was a close friend of Eddie's. I did not bother going into sharing my pains of seeing Sheryl Crow replace me.

While on the date with Eddie, I felt as though he was auditioning me to be his possible girlfriend or a future bride. He asked me questions like do you smoke? Do you go to church? Do you drink? It felt like an audition. However, I did find Eddie to be charming and a gentleman.

Family friend Majestic, on one of his many visits to my apartment, surprised me once by bringing the actor Corey Feldman with him. I first met Corey when I filmed the video with Michael. Corey asked me why I had not attended the premier of Michael's new video, *Moonwalker*. We both became embarrassed and we felt awkward. Corey could not understand why Michael did not invite me and neither could I.

Corey was preparing for a show at the Palace in Hollywood, and he invited me as his guest. It was a fun show and I recall meeting Soileil Moon Frye from the TV show *Punky Brewster*. She innocently asked me to tell Michael hello. I thought how can I do that for her when I can't even call him myself. Some people believed that we were dating or they all thought that we had some sort of connection.

During this time, I was close friends with Matt LaBlanc. This was before he scored a part on the sitcom, *Friends*. We went out a few times, but our physical relationship grew into a friendship. Once his career took off, I felt as though he changed a little. Hollywood and stardom can do that to the best of us. I do recall Matt fully enjoying my DeNiro stories. I guess it was that Italian mano y mano thing that they shared.

TR: Did Michael's mother try to put the two of you in contact with each other again?

TT: It was not too long after that Mrs. Jackson took me with her and the family to one of Michael's shows. It felt good, on one hand, to have his mother in my corner. On the other hand, I went from being a part of the show to watching the show. I guess if I had to go with someone, going with the matriarch of the Star himself was not too shabby.

Majestic picked me up and drove me out to the Jackson home. When I arrived, I waited in the den. Then, more and more people from the Jackson family arrived. You name it; Michael's cousins, aunt's, niece, and nephews arrived. I could not believe how big his family was. There was no way that I could remember all of their names. Rebbie and her three children arrived last and later someone said that she is always the last to show up. Everyone gravitated towards the kitchen. One of Michael's sisters in law asked her son who I was. He looked up at me with these big innocent and shy eyes. At his mom's insistence he answered in the cutest and sweetest voice, "Tatiana Jackson." Everyone cracked up. I was speechless and I was laughing, but the comment made me nervous. However, I will not deny this was my biggest wish and dream. After the

little boy's remark someone said, "That would be nice wouldn't it?" I could not muster up the courage or guts to answer such a question. Although, I agreed within the privacy of my own heart that it would be wonderful.

When we arrived at the stadium, I heard someone mumble, "Hey that is the girl from the video. She is with the Jackson's."

While we were watching the show, I know there were fans wondering why I was not onstage. Towards the end of the show, we left, but it was not soon enough. When we got up to leave, it was the intro of *The Way You Make Me Feel* and I saw Sheryl Crow strutting out. I was not prepared for this. I was not prepared to see her in "the dress" doing my number. It was traumatic. I did not I blame her, though. Why should I? After all, she was just a performer following orders. That is how I saw it. Michaels family and I blamed Dileo. We felt that it was his fault. Then I couldn't help feeling that Michael was in complete control of his personal life. He was calling all the shot's.

As we were walking out, I ran into Corey Feldman who asked me "Why aren't you doing the show?" I said that I did not know. He told me, "You should go backstage after the show and talk to Michael." I did not have much time to explain anything to him because I was trying to keep up with the other family members. I just nodded my head and kept walking. Little did Corey know that this was the initial plan that Mrs. Jackson had first thought of. She invited me so I would have the opportunity to speak with Michael. Yet, we never went backstage. I had a feeling that this was going to happen but I never questioned her about it. I got the feeling that it was a closed issue. Honestly, I felt as though she might have questioned the decision to make the meeting happen.

As they drove me home, I thought about the disappointment of not having spoken with Michael. It was especially disappointing, after seeing Sheryl act out my part and Corey's encouragements for me to go backstage. I was fighting with it all. I tried to make everything look normal on the outside but I was a mess on the inside.

We drove back to the compound and we gathered in the kitchen to discuss the evening's events. There were a few legitimate complaints. For one, no one liked Michael's back-up singers doing the old Jackson 5 material. Two other complaints were about little Jimmy. He had gone from being in a Pepsi commercial with Michael to being incorporated into the show.

Mrs. Jackson also complained that it sickened her that Michael had showered this kid and his parents with gifts. She did not like this and noted that Michael was not spending that much time with his own nieces and nephews. She did not like the way it looked and she was right. She then mentioned that Jimmy even had a tour jacket and none of the nephews had one yet. I cringed inside when the topic came up about how he replaced me in my part. It hurt me. Katharine's biggest complaint, that I thought bothered her the most, was that Michael had moved away from the family home. He had Miko move all of his belongings out of the house for him. He did it when he was on tour and he did not tell anyone. That really hurt her. I shared some of the family's pain and anguish. Jermaine's wife, at the time, Margaret, said that she thought that Dileo was threatened by me and he saw his paychecks going right out the window. Katherine agreed with her. They believed that he was the one controlling Michael. I guess a part of me wanted to find someone else at fault, too. None of us wanted to believe that the real problem was Michael not wanting to talk to us.

Majestic coldly said to me once, "Tatiana you have been traded in for a kid. How does it feel?" Although he was trying to say it in a joking manner, he could be a brutal character at times. He even said, "How does it feel being fucked and not kissed first?" He said this to me after seeing the photos from Michael's 1988 calendar and the 45 single. The products that Michael used my picture to sell. Initially, Majestic was the person to point out to me how comfortable I could be living for the rest of my life, if I were paid a mere penny per copy. Just one cent for the 45 or the calendar, and my life could have been very different. Majestic jokingly called Michael, "A smooth criminal," just like his song. I agreed with him, that when it came to business, Michael was the best. After all, Michael had learned from some of the best in the business.

The investigator, Jerome, and the Jackson's relationship was not going well. From what I heard, he was backstabbing them with deals. That is what Katherine told me. I soon found out that he was shopping for deals for me with a fake demo tape. He was doing the same thing with me that happened to Milli Vanilli.

One time Jerome and I left the Jackson compound to pick something up at his apartment, and he somehow found it appropriate to have a porno channel on while I waited in his living room. This was the moment I ended his chapter.

Chapter Five
Joe Jackson

Before I knew it, Mr. Jackson approached me about representation.

Although I was still working with Terri, everything we did was PR work. Promotional work is good, but I wanted to work. I wanted some real jobs. I will not deny the idea of Joseph Jackson managing me swept me off my feet.

TR: Did you feel that you could trust him?

TT: I had had faith in him, perhaps far more than his own brew. I probably had more faith in him than I should have but I felt that without Joe, none of the Jacksons would have been where they were. His dreams and diligence took them so far. I am a huge believer in destiny and I feel we choose our fate in life. I loved my manager, Terri Hartman, but this offer from Mr. Jackson was one I felt I could not refuse. There was more attached to this deal than Terri or anyone else could imagine. Katherine and Joseph both assured and promised me a visit to the ranch at Neverland Valley to speak to Michael. Therefore, this alone played a big part in me wanting to sign with him. I could not pass on this opportunity.

I went to two different attorneys about the calendar and the 45 single. As misfortune would have it, both were afraid of a case against Jackson productions. They told me to consider myself lucky for having worked with the king. They were too afraid to go up against someone of his stature and power. I was penniless and powerless. I was not going to get anywhere with this. Taking my idol to court and suing him was not in my heart anyway. Nevertheless, I did want to be compensated for what I felt was rightfully mine. Katherine and Joseph seemed so concerned and they wanted to help me professionally and personally. Someone finally wanted to help me and I was obsessed with following their encouragements and suggestions. I felt I was in the best hands imaginable. I loved their son.

Majestic approached me initially about Joseph's interest in managing me and he was also a client, their assistant and houseboy. He was living rent-free in one of their Las Vegas homes.

TR: Did your friends or family feel that it was a good idea to have Joe Jackson as your Manager?

TT: My family agreed that it was a good idea to secure the connection because it could help me clear up my issues with Michael. My agent, Julie, had already messed up and had not contracted a merchandising agreement. Nor had I for that matter. We had only a standard Screen Actors Guild contract that was strictly for the video. Most attorneys feared going up against someone like Michael and most felt I must had signed something that protected their side. I had not knowingly signed such a document.

TR: Did you decide to sign with Joe Jackson?

TT: When I did come to a decision to sign with Joseph, they had me contact one of Joe's representatives – a man named Ben Brown. His claim to fame was that he produced one of Michael's first records, entitled *Big Boy*. He also took pride in the fact that he still owned the rights to the song which must have been an accomplishment in itself. Michael owns everything, and it seemed that Michael wanted the rights to that too.

Mr. Brown and I met Joseph at a restaurant in Encino. Joseph expressed sincere and positive intent as a manager working on my behalf. I left the meeting feeling positive and confident that this was the right move for me. Joseph was charming and funny, and I believed I was in good hands. Joe, in a strange way, reminded me of my own parents. I do not know why, perhaps it was his old school mentality and charm.

Nearly two weeks passed and we were still in the contractual stages. The contract was taking this long to be drawn up. Then, through my ex-boyfriend Angel, I met a female attorney named Terry Bringhaume. She was anxious and hungry to work on a deal involving a name as important as the Jacksons. She had worked on a record deal with Angel and I trusted his judgment. That decision came back to slap me in the face later. She turned out to be so conniving and manipulative, that I did not even know what hit me. My mind does not relate to people who can manipulate and calculate with such evilness. I pride myself in being a good person who would not kill a soul just to get what I want. This girl, well, she would stab you without a thought or pause. I do not know. Maybe nice guys do finish last.

Terry went over the contracts that Mr. Brown sent to her and she agreed to virtually everything. I do not recall her making many changes, if she made any at all. The contract was for five years with a three year extension. I thought eight years was too long, but she told me that it was standard.

The relationship lasted only seven months. I was patient for seven months. Many things went wrong with our partnership and I learned of the lack of respect the entertainment industry has for Joseph and his endeavors. I did not realize this when I signed with him. People were constantly asking me, "Why are you signed with him?" Some even were sarcastic and rude when they found out that he was managing me. They said, "You've got to be kidding?" When it came to business, Michael was highly respected, especially during this time, but his father was not. I was offended when people made negative comments. After all, this was a reflection of my partnership. It was an important time in my career and I did not want any negative light cast on me.

TR: Did Joe get you any work?

TT: There was talk of a movie deal and a recording contract. The first project we were supposed to have done was a movie called *Tracer.* The main character in the film was similar to, La Femme Nikita. I was looking forward to this project and I was very excited about its potential. We even had a meeting with the producers of the film and they hired an acting coach for me to work with. I was on a mental high for months because of this project. I was into the character and the script. I felt confident about its possibilities, and I felt physically capable of doing the part.

A good five months had passed since I first met with the producers and casting agents. Everyday, every week, and every month, Ben Brown had an excuse about the delays. He was constantly telling me to be patient. Joseph left so much in Mr. Brown's hands, that I often questioned who I was really signed with.

I was constantly bringing up the calendar and album to Mr. Jackson reminding him that my financial situation needed to be better. He always assured me that he was going to investigate it and find out firsthand, through Michael, what had happened. I found that I was asking this question so often with no outcome - that I had to question his relationship with his own son. I remembered the family complaining that they could not reach Michael when they wanted or even needed him.

After two or three months, Joe told me that Michael had handpicked me for the part in the video. "What does that have to do

with anything? This I already know," I said. This was not the question at hand. I was trying to not be disrespectful when I asked him, "So, what did he say about the calendar? Or album?" Joe brushed it off and said, "These things take time. I need to do more investigation; I'll be talking to Michael again." He was stating that he had Michael on the telephone, which is supposedly hard to do, and

he did not use that opportunity to ask him about the things regarding me, his client? When was I going to get an answer?

TR: Were you working at all then? Were you still going to auditions?

TT: During this time there was an audition coming up for an *LA Gear* commercial. Michael had a big campaign with them at the time, and my agent wanted me to go up for it. I did audition, but they did not pick me. Several clients did not pick me. They said, "She has that Michael Jackson Girl image." This worked against me a lot.

I auditioned for Pepsi and was told that they already had Michael and did not need another reminder of his image.

I also had a Coke audition and was told that they could not use me because I was a reflection of Michael which would be a conflict of interest. It seemed that my relationship with Michael Jackson was working against me all the time. It was hard enough that I had a look that makes it difficult to know what 'category' to place me in. Now I had another obstacle that worried me. I had the "Michael Jackson Girl" image strapped to my back. I even heard at music video auditions that "We're sorry. We are looking for a new face, and you are a little too famous." Some of the videos were for new recording artists. Their managers or the label were concerned that I was too recognizable. They thought that I was going to steal the thunder from their artist altogether.

There was a new band on the scene during this time called, the Dan Reed Network. They wanted to use me in one of their videos, but I believe it was not booked because of finances. Just the same, the lead singer wrote a song about me, and he named it after me. I was honored to say the least, and if you are still out there, I thank you! I was deeply touched and I loved the song.

During this time, my mother called and told me that my first dance Teacher, Beatriz DeParis, was organizing an Alumni Salute for me in Clearwater, Florida. It was to be a special dinner in my honor saluting my achievements. They wanted to present me with the key to the city of Clearwater which is my hometown. I was honored beyond words but I did wonder why they had picked me. I felt as though this was an honor that should be given to someone who had accomplished much more than I had. I felt this was premature and I just did not quite feel worthy.

The event was all prearranged and planned so I was obligated to follow through on their time schedule. Mr. Jackson scheduled an important meeting for me at the same time, and my teacher was very annoyed at the thought of me not attending. I received so much press promoting the event that classmates from many of my classes called to say hello and congratulations. I even had relatives that I didn't know call to say hello! It was all interesting and odd. The press was calling my mother and asking her questions. It was weird to be in my skin sometimes. I cannot say that I was always comfortable with it. You see, I had not changed, but it seemed the way people felt about me and treated me had changed.

When I arrived for the dinner, I could not believe my eyes. There was a full house - the room was packed! My teacher and the mayor presented me with the key to the city of Clearwater.

Me at the Jackson House

Then the audience had the floor and started to ask me questions. It was a surreal experience. When I accepted my award, I did not have anything planned, or prepared, and my speech was natural and unrehearsed. The Gulf Coast Ballet Company ended the awards with a beautiful performance.

At the Jackson House

When I returned to Los Angeles I helped with a children's charity that Mr. Jackson was involved in. I drove to Las Vegas – the event site – with Mr. Brown with another one of Joseph's clients; a small Asian girl named Mihoko who was a singer. We checked into a hotel for the first evening with plans to spend the night after the event at the Jackson's Vegas home.

When we arrived at the house, Mihoko walked in and immediately rushed to one of the rooms and put her bags down. Mrs. Jackson complained to me about this saying that she planned for me to stay in this room Mihoko had chosen. I found Mihoko to be a bit disrespectful to the Matriarch, but she was good at kissing up to Mr. Jackson. It was obvious that he liked the attention. I could not help but feel there was more to this relationship than met the eye and I could tell Mrs. Jackson felt the same.

Later that evening, Majestic and I watched television with Katherine. I felt more comfortable around her than Joseph. He was a bit too hard and stern at times. Majestic asked me, "Wouldn't she be a great mother-in-law?" and he was right. She always appeared to have a soft and sweet side to her. She loves to play board games and is especially good at scrabble.

The entire group was scheduled for a charity event at a park located near the Jackson house. The event was not at all what I expected. I had the feeling I was at a family barbecue. This was my first visit to Las Vegas and I was very excited about seeing the nightlife — the bright lights, casinos, and slot machines.

Mrs. Jackson did not go with us on my first adventure of Vegas and we planned to go back to the hotel after the event.

When we arrived at the hotel, I ran right into Miko Brando. This was the first time I saw him since my *Bad* tour days and we shared a brief moment of awkward pleasantries. It did not occur to me until later that Michael was probably in town and staying in the same hotel. Once this hit me, I knew that someone would tell Michael that I was in the hotel. After all, Miko was his personal assistant. I mentioned this to Mr. & Mrs. Jackson but they didn't have a comment.

On my last day there, Majestic told Katherine that I wanted to see a Vegas show. Katherine and I started talking about the possibility of going to a show together, and the two of us staying another day. Joseph walked in as we were having this conversation and unfortunately, he did not like it one bit. Before I knew it, Joseph requested that Mr. Brown and I join him in the room in which I was staying. Joseph told me that he was the one who had initially invited me - not Katie - and that I should have asked him about this first. He also said that if I wanted to come back with her on another trip that was fine, but that I was not going to add an evening with her or be staying another night. I am extremely sensitive and because of the way he handled this, with such a harsh tone in his voice, I started to choke up a bit and cry. Oddly enough, I somehow felt that I understood the inspiration behind Janet Jackson's hit song *Control*.

I felt I was experiencing her words firsthand.

When the three of us came out of the room, where I had been chewed out, I did my best not to lose it and not cry in front of Katherine, but I felt the tears welling up. Sitting next to her, I wanted to let it all go and cry in her arms. I trusted and felt so comforted by her and I wanted to stay another day with her. In the end, we both submitted to the pressure. We did not say a word to each other.

TR: What made you decide to submit (in your words) to Joseph? He was not your father and you were a grown Woman...

TT: I followed through with Joseph's original plan to leave the following day. I assumed Katherine knew why. It was clear who controlled everything. It was obvious that Katherine took the backseat on this as well.

About one week after we returned to LA, there was a big party held at the Jackson home in Encino. It was a celebration for several of Joseph's clients and projects, myself included. One of his 'babies' was a soft drink product called *Joe Cola.*

To my complete surprise, my ex-attorney, Terry Bringhaum was at the party. She was the one who had admitted to me a week earlier that she was elated in meeting me because she only wanted to get to the Jacksons. She said to me, "I never cared about you as a client. You were my link to get to them. I always wanted to be connected to the Jacksons." Well, now she was connected.

Majestic told me that she was working on several projects with Joseph. She was even working on one that involved Michael. I could not believe it. I knew Katherine disliked her, and did not trust her. Majestic told me that Katherine had asked him, "Where did Tatiana find her? Why did she ever bring her around?" The whole thing was such a joke. My attorney had used me to get to my future manager. Then, when he became my manager, she admitted to me that she had used me to get to them and then jumped off my ship to join his. This whole thing made me sick! I was so disappointed! The whole situation was such a farce. I was frustrated beyond words about my career. It seemed obvious that if she had admittedly used me to get to the Jackson family that she had not negotiated my contract to protect me. I realized that I signed my career and my life away. This was when I realized it was all a joke. It was time to do something. As difficult as it would be, it was time to move on.

TR: Did you have any income at all then? How did you pay your bills?

TT: During this time, I got a job at the *China Club*. Everyone in the industry went to this hot spot. It was "The Club." I was the coat check girl, so I greeted all the guests and knew who was there. There were many celebrities who were regulars; Sylvester Stallone, Eddie Murphy, Paul Stanley from *KISS*, Richard Greico, David Bowie, Julian Lennon — the list of celebrities was long. The China Club was the first place that an artist like Bruce Willis would 'jam' with an artist like Elton John. It was a fun place to work. Mondays and Thursdays were the hottest nights – the nights that celebrities showed up and jammed live onstage.

One night, Scott Baio came in and flirted heavily with me. I could not believe it! He was overwhelming and I could not even flirt back because I was in awe of him! He was just a dream to me. I always had a crush on him but I was too shy to respond to him. I think he got the impression that he did not faze me or that I did not like him. However, it was just the opposite. He was all that!

After working at the club for about a month, I invited Mr. Jackson and Mr. Brown to be my guests. After all, it was Joseph's idea that I get a normal job. My friends at the club, however, felt that as my manager, he should have had me working as an actress. They did not think that I should have to work as a coat check girl. People wondered why my career was standing still when in fact it should have been on the rise.

We arranged to meet at the club on my night off. I was not told who would be picking me up; I hoped it would be Joseph, since he was my manager. He told me he wanted to support my efforts especially since he advised me to get a job to supplement my income until one of our projects took off.

Early on, the evening's wires got crossed. Joseph, Ben and even Terry went to the club without me. I planned the entire evening, and I ended up at home alone wondering what had happened to my guests. I guess the joke was on me. Mr. Jackson later complained to me how Terry had to wait alone at the club entrance. I could not believe what I was hearing. I had put his name, and mine, on the guest list plus two guests. Terry was his guest and Mr. Brown was mine. At this point, I realized what and who his priorities were.

Terry's newfound relationship with Mr. Jackson was a conflict of interest and I decided to cut off contact with her. After I signed with Mr. Jackson, and prior to the party, her attitude towards me could only be described as nasty. I had witnessed a major change in her. When we first met, she appeared to be sweet and kind to me. Once she got in with Mr. Jackson, and began working on deals with him, she became very dictatorial. Majestic told me that she went to Las Vegas as Joseph's guest. I knew that things were not right with my camp. My ship was sinking and I had no answers.

I met Rob and Fab from the group Milli Vanilli around this time. Rob and I became friends and even dated for a brief spell. He could not believe, like many others, that I was under management with Joseph Jackson. Rob told me about a meeting he and Fab had with

Joseph and Joseph supposedly approached them with a music deal. Rob offered to help me get out of my contract with Joseph, but instead I would opt for someone else's advice and guidance. That someone else was Robert DeNiro.

ポルシェをかけた日、わたしは翔んだ。

Chapter Six
Desperately Seeking DeNiro

On a night off from the China Club, I received a phone call from one of my bosses Danny. He was also one of the owners of the club. He told me that he wanted me to come in the following evening – also my night off. When I asked why, he said that Robert DeNiro had been in to the club and had seen my head shot hanging in the office. I gave this photo to my bosses when they hired me. Danny said that Robert wanted to meet me. I was silent and I just sat there listening to him. I guess because I was keeping cool about this information. Danny got persistent saying, "Hey! I am talking about Robert DeNiro here. You should make an effort to meet him. He could help your career. You never know. Maybe he will put you in one of his films!" I did not jump all over the idea. Antonio had warned me about Bobby years before saying, "Tatiana don't you ever get involved with Bobby. He is Toukies man, and she'll kick your butt." Bobby and Toukie Smith had been an item for years.

Toukie was at one time a model. I also did not trust the idea that DeNiro would put me in one of his films. I did not want a part just because someone liked me or wanted to help me. I did not trust or believe it was that simple or easy. I agreed to show up and I brought one of my girlfriends, Angela Alvarado, who was an actress and a beautiful tall Puerto Rican girl. We had some things in common. She was a former model, and she was making the transition from modeling to acting. Her first big break was the film *Salsa*.

When Angela and I arrived at the club, we asked Danny about DeNiro at least three times. Danny acted busy, and as if he did not know what I was talking about. By the fourth inquiry, he said that he was not sure if DeNiro had even arrived yet. Angela and I thought that was too odd. The owner of the Club would know if one of the world's greatest actors was in his club or not. A few seconds after asking Danny about DeNiro, Angela and I spotted him at a table sitting with another guy and two other women. How weird that Angela and I were asking Danny if DeNiro had arrived and there he sat in the roped off, VIP Section with a small party of three. I also thought it was odd that two other women were there since Danny had made it clear he had invited me on some kind of date. This kind of scenario was somewhat typical stuff that happens in Hollywood.

When the women finally left, Angela and I introduced ourselves and joined DeNiro and his male guest. We told him honestly that we had been asking Danny about his whereabouts and Bobby acted as though he did not know who Danny was, saying, "Danny? Who is Danny? I don't know a Danny." Angela knew that this was some kind of game and she said to me, "Oh this is such total bullshit T! Now suddenly he does not know who Danny is!" DeNiro did not catch on to what she said nor did he comment on Angela's remark. I was so glad I had Angela with me. She was the kind of friend you knew had your back in times of real need. She did as much on many occasions. Ironically, Angela starred in a film with Bobby fourteen years later called, *Showtime*. I am sure she thought about the days she shared with me at the China Club. I doubt though that she reminded Bobby that she was the girl who remarked, "This is total bullshit T." I was happy to see that she had accomplished one of her dreams as I remember her saying that she wanted to work with him someday. I believe that when you conceive a dream you can achieve it. We can will whatever we want in life. We just have to foresee the dream and work hard. I am proud and happy that she was able to bring one of her dreams to fruition.

TR: So what did you and Robert DeNiro talk about?

TT: We made small talk for a while and I told DeNiro that I admired and respected his work. For some reason I told him that I never wanted to change the image I held of him. My instinct made me say this to him. It was almost like a prediction, somehow. Unfortunately, when I look back on tarnished relations and disappointments I have had with people, I was correct in saying this to him. I did not care about his status as the world's biggest star. The bottom line was that he was just another man made in God's likeness.

Bobby told me with complete confidence that he was going to phone me later at home to see if I got in all right. I told him that he did not even have my phone number yet. Then I thought, how cocky and arrogant. He assured me that he did have it, and that he would call. Angela and I ended up staying at the club for at least an hour dancing and socializing.

TR: Did he call you that night as he said he would?

TT: When I got home, it only took five minutes for the phone to ring. Yes, it was DeNiro. Somehow, I was still stunned that he called so quickly, even though he did tell me that he was going to. Danny never admitted to me that he gave him my number, but then again, he never admitted to me that he was in the club either. On one hand, I was touched that he was calling, but on another hand, I felt like Danny had 'arranged' the situation much like he would with a call girl or something. I mean, why didn't DeNiro just ask me for my number himself? Why did the two of them act as though they didn't know each other? I felt like a Christmas goose that was being prepared for the feast.

TR: What did you and DeNiro talk about during your phone conversation?

TT: During the phone conversation, Bobby was kind and sweet. He said that he was pleased to see that I got home all right, and that he wanted to get together with me sometime to talk. He asked if he could call me the next day. I told him that I would be home in the afternoon and to call me then.

The following morning at 10:00 a.m., he called. It took me by surprise a bit, but it did make an impression on me. It was a sweet good morning, hello call.

DeNiro called again later in the afternoon. He told me that he was headed back to New York for a few days but that he would love to take me out for lunch when he returned. I agreed, and when he returned, he came to my home to pick me up. I then lived in the San Fernando Valley area of Los Angeles. When he walked into my apartment, he immediately noticed a huge painting that Antonio had done of me. This was a special piece to me and when *People* magazine wrote an article on Antonio in 1982, they included the painting. Bobby recognized the painting right away and I knew that he would, because his girlfriend Toukie had also worked with Antonio. In fact, she and I had worked together on a job with Antonio that was for the designer Fiorucci.

My cat, Magic Michael, made his presence known, darting out of nowhere and jumping on Robert. I thought it was funny and I cracked up. When Robert pointed out the Antonio, he mumbled that he was familiar with his work. I waited to see if he was going to make any comment about Toukie and their relationship. I did not know where there relationship stood but he never said anything about it. Antonio's advice to me about not getting involved with Toukie's man cruised through my memory bank. Antonio had warned me, as if he knew my turn with DeNiro would come someday. It was a known fact that Bobby loved women of color. DeNiro was not the greatest conversationalist, but he was sweet and charming. For some crazy reason, I felt comfortable enough with him to disclose my problems and my concerns about my contract with Michael's father. There were moments when he looked into my eyes and I felt his concern was genuine.

TR: Where did you and DeNiro go on your date?

TT: We went to *Residuals*. It was a little place frequented by people in the industry and near my apartment. It was a very nice first date. He was concerned that someone was going to recognize him, but no one did. As odd as that sounds, he was not in disguise at all. He did not have a hat on, or dark sunglasses. Our waitress didn't even know who he was. He did wear reading glasses, but they just made him look nerdy and unrecognizable.

On our second date, Robert took me out to a Japanese restaurant in downtown Chinatown. It was a pleasant date and we began a friendship.

The following day I called a friend of mine – an attorney named Garry Walterstein. I met him when I had been under management with

Terri Hartman and worked with him during the time I was doing the demo records. I asked Gary for advice and assistance about my contract with Joe Jackson. I got two different attorney's advice, and both of them had said that the agreement was binding, and it would not be easy to get out of it. I worried myself sick about it. The last thing I wanted was to be stuck into a contract with someone who did nothing for my career. Close to six months had passed and Mr. Jackson and Ben Brown had done nothing for my career. The only thing I received was ridicule and sarcastic comments from people about my management and my contract. I was beginning to realize that I had been better off being with my last manager, Terri Hartman. She actually did a good job for me and I would eventually thank her for everything she had done. The main reason that I signed with Joe was that there were so many unanswered questions that I had for Michael. Answers that Joe had promised me he would find out the answers to.

Majestic relayed a message to me that he heard that Michael's response to me signing with Joseph was, "She can't be that stupid!" I could not believe what I was hearing. "Michael said that?" I asked? I never knew for sure if he did or not. I never knew what the truth was. When I asked Majestic, "When and where did you hear that?" he would not disclose how he knew. I was getting fed up with all the rumors and the gossip. It seemed to me there was some communication between Michael and his parents but none of them would put me in touch with him as they promised me. Joseph's reply always was, "These thing's take time."

Bobby and I talked again around this time as he was in town for a few weeks. He was staying at the *Beverly Hills Hotel* and he phoned one evening, insistent that I come and visit him. He asked me about the contract giving me the impression that he could find someone to help me, or that he would help me find an attorney. I was at home with a girlfriend named Kookie, and neither one of us felt like moving. We were comfortable at home together, just chatting. I told Bobby that I did not feel like going out, but he was very persistent. "Oh come on! Just for a while," he said. Most women, I guess, would think I was crazy or out of my mind to say no to someone like DeNiro. I think that was one reason he liked me. I was a challenge for him and my guess is most women fell at his feet.

Michael was the one who held the key to my heart. When I look back on everything now, I missed a few good men because of my feelings for Michael. I have no regrets though. You have to be open and ready for things as they come. Open I was not, and ready? Mentally preoccupied was more like it.

TR: Did you go and meet him or did you decline?

TT: I told Bobby I would think about it and get right back to him. As soon as we hung up, the phone rang and it was Bobby again pleading, "Just for a little while, bring your friend too. I don't care," he said.

Kookie and I arrived at the hotel around 9:30 p.m. Bobby had a friend with him who announced about fifteen to twenty minutes later that he needed a ride to his car. Of course, he directed this question to my girlfriend Kookie. She and I just looked at each other like, okay, but we had expected the set up. Kookie was concerned and wanted to know if I wanted her to stay, asking me if I would be okay. I reassured her to go ahead and that I would take a cab home. I did feel comfortable with Robert and I did need to speak with him.

Once Kookie left, we spoke about the contract which I brought with me. Robert asked, "Why do you even have a manager for acting? All you need is an agent." He argued this fact, insisting why, and why Joe Jackson? I remember Bobby having a sarcastic expression on his face acting out the craziness of it all; saying that Mr. Jackson's status and profile was low on the industry's totem poll of respect. He told me that Michael was a great entertainer and performer and that he was even weird but that Joe was a total joke. I agreed that I was not knowledgeable about what I gotten myself into although, it did bother me a bit that he called Michael weird. I somehow agreed and I thought that he might be right. After all, geniuses are a bit weird. He mentioned knowing Dileo, Michael's Manager, and how they were friends. I reminded Bobby about the calendar and album and that I had not been paid for any of it. He then brushed it all off by telling me that I needed an attorney's help, DUH! It was obvious that it was all too much for him to be bothered with at this moment.

Before I knew what hit me, Bobby wrapped his arms around me in a lock and hold position. I felt as though an octopus was attacking me. I demanded that he let go of me or I was going to punch him. He started laughing and he let go of me. I started to see his real intentions and I told him that this was all a farce. He did not care about helping me. He suddenly got serious, and he apologized. However, that lasted for only five minutes and it was back to "Octopussy." His arms wrapped around me again and I was a little enraged and I threatened to leave if he did not shape up. He stopped for long enough that it made me decide to stay a few minutes more. Bobby then excused himself and he said that he wanted to change into something more comfortable. Suddenly, I felt as though I was in an old movie scene and that he was reading a line from a script. You know, usually the woman is the one that says ,"Let me go change into something more comfortable." Within seconds, he came prancing out in a thick white *Beverly Hills Hotel* robe. He assured me that nothing was going to happen, and that he was not going to harm me. He said all of this as he was pulling me into the bedroom. I assured him back by saying; "Oh, I know. Nothing is going to happen because I will kick your ass, if you try anything." Suddenly, I was in my tough girl New York mode. He laughed and found it all amusing, and I thought he was being silly and playful. Never did I feel threatened or scared, if anything Bobby amused me with it all.

Suddenly Bobby jumped onto the bed and started acting like a little kid, jumping up and down. I could not believe my eyes. Here was the Great Robert DeNiro jumping up and down on a bed flashing me as his robe flew open. Somehow, I just could not get into the moment. I had arrived with a mission in mind, to find a resolution to this dam contract. I am a Taurus and we can be serious at times. This was one of those times. I demanded that he call me a cab. I told him that this was all ridiculous and a joke! When Bobby hung up the phone from calling me a cab, I asked him, "What would you do if there was a fire right now?" Until this day, I have no idea why or where that question came from. Bobby replied, "Well I guess I would run out of here!" I then replied, everyone who saw you would say, "There goes DeNiro, what a little weenie!" Yeah, I know, it was a bad choice of words, but you have to understand, I was frustrated with these games. I wanted some advice and help with this contract. I was not in the moment or mood for this playful crap and I felt he was making light of it all, and he was. Why I chose the word "Weenie" I do not know. It just flew right out of my mouth. As I used the word, I meant he was the weenie, but I am sure he thought I was speaking about his anatomy. That was not what I meant! That was completely intact, in all honesty. I made the comment to distract him and turn his motor off. It had worked and I was on my way home.

TR: Were you not attracted to him? Is that why you did not want to talk about more than the contract?

TT: I found Bobby very attractive but my head was just not in the mental place that he was. I guess he viewed me as playing hard to get, but I was not. He was beginning to do exactly what I initially feared and had expressed at our first meeting. He was tarnishing my respect for him and changing the image that I held for him.

TR: Did you talk to him again after that night?

TT: He phoned me several times the following day, as I assumed he would. I screened my calls until I was ready to discuss what had happened and when we did speak, he was extremely apologetic and a true gentleman. All was forgiven. I had agreed to call him later that afternoon but something came up, and I did not get home until much later. Keep in mind that this was the day before cell phones and the luxury of constantly being in touch. So, when I did finally come home there were five messages from Bobby — one after another and with each message he grew more and more angry. By the fifth message, my mouth was hanging open from the shock because of his tone and the words he was using.

TR: What did he say?

TT: The first message was upbeat and friendly. He said "Hey Tatiana its Bobby. Call me when you get in."

The second message he said, "Hey, it's Bobby again. I am just calling to see if you are in yet. Call me, I'll be here."

In the third message he said, "Yeah, it's me again. Where are you? You said you would call me and I am waiting to hear from you. Call me when you get in."

By the fourth call, he got a bit irate and his tone of voice was not pleasant. He said, "Hey, where the fuck are you? I can't fucking believe you haven't called me yet. You said you would call me, and I think it is pretty fucken rude of you to keep me waiting. You said you would call."

The fifth call was the final straw, and it blew me away. He said, "I just can't believe that you haven't fucken called me. Do you wanna see what I can do for you? Is that it? That's it! You wanna see what I can do for your career? I can't fucken believe that you haven't called me back yet."

TR: Did you finally call him back?

TT: I immediately called him and gave him a piece of my mind. I apologized for not calling him as I promised, but told him he had no right to leave such profane messages on my machine, and that I wasn't his wife or girlfriend and I didn't owe him anything.

Before I knew it, we were making plans to go to the movies. We went to see *Pretty Woman*. After the film, I told Bobby that unlike the character in the movie I hadn't found my prince charming in him. I broke it off with him. Call me stupid, but I didn't have feelings for him and I was not about to use him or any other man to try to further my career. I felt confident enough in myself and I always wanted to succeed on my own merit. I have tons of pride, and a healthy amount of self-respect. When I got out of his Mercedes, I never looked back.

Chapter Seven
A Raspberry Beret Birthday

My 29th birthday was on April 22nd, 1989. I celebrated it with a group of friends at *Club 20-20* in Century City. Someone at my party told me that Prince just arrived. I figured since it was my birthday, I was going to ask him to dance with me which is how I met and danced with the artist formerly known as Prince.

To back up a bit, my friend Craig astounded all of us with his Michael Jackson moves. He had them down and it was like watching the "Bad One" himself. I walked over to Princes table and I politely said to his bodyguards that I wanted to ask Prince for a dance. I had to go thorough them first because there were several of them blocking the front of his table. Prince was sitting down and his bodyguards parted and let me enter. It was like the parting of the Red Sea. We were all having a great time but I think my friends were amazed when I walked over to Prince's table and I politely said to his bodyguards that I wanted to dance with him. I told Prince that it was my birthday. I said to him, "If I could have one birthday wish it would be to dance with you." He nodded his head yes. He is a man of few words. We tore up the dance floor to Madonna's song, *Like a Prayer.* The entire club was gawking at us. I caught my friend Kookie, trying to take a snapshot as we danced. Prince's bodyguards stepped in front of her and stopped her dead in her tracks. I was disappointed because she was not quick enough.

Prince walked me back to my table. He said that I had an open invitation to join him at his table. I quietly agreed to go meet him there in a few minutes. After all, it was my birthday! My friends and guests gathered around me. They started asking me if I knew Prince. I replied, “No, I just met him.” They were all so surprised because I casually walked over to him and asked him if he would dance with me. I did it as if we already knew each other. Kookie kept saying how disappointed she was because they would not let her take a picture of Prince. My girlfriend Audra was so mad at herself because she had not made it to my birthday party. She was a huge Prince fan.

After blowing out my candles and opening my gifts, I excused myself and went to Prince’s table to join him. When our drinks arrived, he offered me a taste of his drink. He had a Virgin Pina’ Colãda. I said, “No thank you, but can I have your cherry?” Prince gave me this wide-eyed, shocked expression. He took it as a sexual innuendo. I said that was not my intention and we started cracking up. Prince liked innuendos and double meanings, so he enjoyed that.

As this exciting evening progressed, Prince asked me to join him in his limo. He wanted to take me for a ride. He walked out ahead of me and told me that one of his guys would be waiting for me to take me to his limo. After fifteen minutes or so, I was like Cinderella leaving the ball. His ‘people’ were dashing me off to my carriage before it turned into a pumpkin.

When I walked up to the long, white stretch limo, I stopped in my tracks. I wanted to make a mental note of this magical moment. The glow of the evening light bounced off the limo’s frame. It looked like something from a fairy tale or a Hollywood movie. I felt like Cinderella and this was the most wonderful birthday I have ever had in my life.

TR: So where did you and Prince go?

TT: We just rode around Westwood all-night. We were listening to some of his new music on his demo. He asked me what I thought about his new stuff. One of the songs was a demo of Sheena Easton singing a song that Prince had produced. I told him that I had met her once and said hello but she ignored me and that I hated that crap! I added I couldn’t stand snobs. Anyway, I loved his new stuff.

TR: So what did you do at the end of the night?

TT: I was not ready for this night to end, but we had been driving around for a few hours. He invited me to his hotel — the *Sunset Marquee* in Westwood. I questioned the thought of going there with him. After all, we had just met. But we were both having such a wonderful time together and neither one of us was tired.

When I entered his room, I took a mental picture of everything. How neat he was, the artwork, even the smell of the air. Although this was a hotel, Prince was living there; making it his home.

He showed me around and we walked down a short hallway that led to the bedroom. I recall staring at a painting that hung above the bed. The detail was so small and faint that from a distance I could not make sense of it. As I got closer, I saw that it was all nude women intertwined together. He told me, "Don't get too close it might damage your eyes." I told him that it did not frighten or faze me. Prince was a musical genius and he intrigued me. He walked me towards his closet and it was amazing! It was just awesome beyond words. Before me hung dozens and dozens of outfits. I was dazzled by the colors, textures, bold prints, and designs. For every outfit, there was a matching pair of boots. His closet was the bomb! It was unlike anything I have ever laid my eyes on. He told me, "Curiosity killed the cat." I stepped in his closet further and said, "Yeah, well the cat had nine lives." He got a kick out of my quick come back. He asked me, "Would you like it if I dressed you up in my clothes sometime." I told him that would be cool, but I thought his pants would be excessively too short for me. He is only 5'4" and I am 5'7". However, I tried on one of his boots, and it was a perfect fit.

He started telling me a story and started it out by saying, "Yah know, when I was little. Well, I'm still little." Before he could finish, I started laughing so hard. I though I was going to bust a gut from laughing so hard. I thought it was great that he could joke and laugh at himself and make light of his small frame. I thought it was cool for a few seconds anyway. Suddenly, I stopped laughing because of this expression on his face. There was immediate silence. He had this look on his face as to say, "I can make fun of myself but you cannot." Prince is a Gemini and I soon learned that his moods switched on and off like a light switch.

His bathroom bewildered me. Laid out were an endless amount of make-up and toiletries. Any girl would have been jealous. The vanity layout was so beautifully arranged. You could view every piece of lip liner, mascara, and eyeliner. He had more make-up and perfume than any woman I knew.

We went back into the living room, and he asked me if I was hungry. I was, and minutes later, everything I ordered was in double amounts. Prince did not touch any of it. I thought it was odd that he did not have anything to eat, especially since he ordered so much. Why did he order so much if he was not going to eat? Did he think I was a pig?

After I ate, Prince and I sat Indian style on the living room floor. We just sat and talked. I had a top on that was strapless, and out of nowhere, Prince yanked my top down. He did it in a playful manner as if he was still a little kid. A spoiled brat was more like it. I did not flinch when he did it and he asked, "I thought you said you were shy?" That was the last topic of our conversation. It was his playful test for me. He wanted to see how I would react and see how I would respond to it. He asked me inquisitively, "Do you ever caress them or play with them?" I could not believe that he was asking me this and I quickly answered, "No!" I know I started blushing and I laughed it off. He then asked me, "Well why not? They're beautiful." The conversation quickly switched from my beautiful boobs, to Vanity. She was the lead singer of his girl group Vanity 6. I told him that I knew Vanity and knew that her real name was Denise Matthews. We met in Tokyo when we both were signed with *Zoli*. It was during that time she was working with Prince in the studio. They were working on a demo for the single *Nasty Girls*. I was staying in her New York apartment and she had given me strict instructions not to answer a red phone. She was the only person that could answer it so I assumed that Prince called her on that phone. After I told Prince the story he said, "Oh, that Vanity!"

It was already 5:00 am and we were still talking. We were like two kids defying the limits and boundaries of time. We did not want to go to sleep. I felt comfortable with him and I was having a ball. He asked me if I wanted to sleep over and I agreed. Before I knew it, prince handed me a beautiful pair of silk pajamas. The entire scenario was out of the ordinary for me, but we were having fun and there was such trust and comfort that I reasoned with myself it was okay to spend the night with him.

I changed into the pajamas, and I asked him what he was going to put on. He told me, "These are my pajamas," —telling me the black lycra cat suit with half of the waist missing were his pajamas for the evening. There was a chain attached to the cat suit that dangled from his waist from one side of his body to the other. I thought, Well, You go ahead with yah bad self. Prince, Do your thing! Geniuses are odd. He is a genius and he is odd. We curled up in bed like kittens, and simply fell asleep. It was as sweet and innocent as that. It took me forever to fall asleep though. I could not believe that I was snuggled up in bed with one of the greatest artists of that time. In a way, Prince was viewed as Michael's musical rival.

TR: How are the two of them different?

TT: Michael was the Peter Pan squeaky-clean one, and Prince was the sexually overt one. They were like night and day, but they were both geniuses and incredible to observe. Prince admired and respected Michael.

TR: Did you talk to Prince again after your birthday night?

TT: A few days later Prince called me and invited me to a concert. The group Guy was performing at the *Universal Amphi Theater*. Prince asked me if I would mind if the press took a few pictures of us together. I said that it would not bother me in the least and that it was part of the deal. I felt that Prince was concerned about the media putting their own twisted spin on us and it was also out of concern and respect for Michael. He believed, like most, there was something between us. The show was incredible and Teddy Riley was awesome! Prince admired his work.

After the show, we rode around the lot of Universal and Prince asked if I wanted to drive the limo for fun. I passed because I did not even have my license yet. I didn't admit to him that I did not want to crash the limo or be responsible for it.

That night I wore a silver belt buckle that spelled out LOVE in bold letters. It was similar to a belt Madonna had worn in the early 80's that read Boy Toy. Several times during the night, Prince complimented me on it. He told me that he wanted one that spelled out Gemini. He wanted his in gold, and mine was in silver.

Prince and I spoke several times by phone and at odd hours. It seemed we both had a late night schedule. We spoke many times at 3:00 or 4:00 in the morning. Once he called me and when I answered he said,

"I bet you're sorry you gave me your number huh?" I reassured him and said, "Not at all, I'm a night owl."

A few weeks went by and I ran into him at *Vertigo*, a popular nightclub. Prince asked me to join him as he sat surrounded by three other women. Sometime during the evening, I asked him if he was seeing or dating anyone. He replied something like, "I don't have any! I have many. " Suddenly, he turned into Dr. Jeckel and his mood changed. He left me standing on the dance floor alone.

At the time, I was working on a special surprise gift for him. I had called a friend in New York and asked him to make a gold belt buckle that spelled out GEMINI. This is what Prince said that he wanted. I did all this for someone who left me on a dance floor alone. Gemini's are strange. They do have two sides to their personalities. Prince did show me his gratitude by wearing the buckle in his video *Batdance*. In the video, he plays a character named Gemini. The video was for the movie *Batman*.

Chapter Eight
The B.R.E. Awards

May 11th, 1989 - The creative consultant for the Black Radio Exclusive Awards show, Ingrid Woodson, called me. She said that Michael was being awarded the outstanding achievement award in the "Pop, Rock and Soul" categories. He won the "Triple Crown Award" which is the highest honor of the evening. Ingrid said that she wanted me to be part of the show — to present the award to Michael. I was honored that they had considered me and the invitation gave me new hope and lifted my spirits. Finally, it seemed I would have an opportunity to see and speak to Michael. I looked at this as if it was God's doing.

I spoke with the producers several times over the next two weeks. What I did not know at the time was that Ingrid was familiar with all the industry gossip that surrounded Michael and me. She also knew about me being fired from the *Bad Tour*. Ingrid told me that she felt that an injustice was committed towards me and that she had heard and felt that Michael cared very much about me. Ingrid felt I was the underdog. She said that there must have been a misunderstanding between us and wanted to help. As I listened to her over the phone saying all of this to me, I felt deeply touched that she cared so much and wanted to help me. I was beginning to regard her as a "Guardian Angel" of sorts.

Opposite: The B. R. E. Awards

It is rare in Hollywood to find people who care enough to want to do something positive to help you, especially behind the scenes. Ingrid's view on the situation surrounding Michael and me was very rare. Her views reminded me of what his parents and my parents thought. Ingrid said that she heard from many people in the industry that Michael cared for me, but she felt his professional camp had taken control of the situation by brainwashing him and telling him lies about me. Ingrid wanted to give us the opportunity to work together again and she wanted us to get together and speak one on one.

I invited Joe Jackson as my guest. Joe said, "We already know about the show and the entire family has tickets to it. I will check my schedule and see what else I have to do. I will try to come." He did not seem enthused and his lack of interest hurt my feelings.

The show was held at the *Universal Amphitheater* on May 28th, 1989. I put a lot of thought and preparation into my image for the award show. I wanted to emulate the old days of Hollywood, when the stars were truly glamorous. I used Rita Hayworth as my inspiration and I wore the long white gown Terri Hartman had bought for me. I styled it with long white satin gloves and with silver pumps that sparkled with rhinestones. It was glamour at its finest.

When I arrived at the theater, I reported in to the producers and we had dinner in the green room. There was nearly an hour before the show started and the producers had me wait with the other performers and presenters in a special waiting room, separating me from the two friends I had brought as my guests.

Ben Brown, my assistant manager, had come in Joe Jackson's place. This really disappointed me and while Ben and I waited around, someone from the media snapped a few photos of us and then teamed me up with Little Richard. He is one of the original creators and innovators of rock and roll. He inspired Elvis, Prince, Michael, and Terence Trent Darby. To me, Little Richard is the King of Rock n Roll. As a little girl, he captivated me. His good looks, style, hair, and the way he tore up a piano was too cool, and unlike anyone else out there. When Prince came along it was like de' javu.' To me, Prince was the spitting image of Little Richard but in a different time. Little Richard was way ahead of himself.

We finished the photos and it was close to show time. I was on stand-by and I started getting nervous. When I was walking backstage, I felt confident that things would finally be resolved for me, and that I would finally have some peace of mind after speaking to Michael.

As I waited to present the award, I dazed out onto the stage and watched the singing group "Surface" perform. Quincy Jones was standing not too far away from me and he too was a part of the special presentation for Michael.

My original entrance was to be stage right, but just a few minutes before, Ingrid told me to walk across to stage left, changing the original plan. As we got half way across, I heard someone saying something through a walkie-talkie to the person escorting me, who was Ingrid's husband. It was so muffled that I could not make complete sense of the voice at the other end. What I did hear was "Michael something, something... Tatiana." I was so excited at the time and I was walking with a big smile on my face. I was so elated about being there and having this opportunity to talk to and see Michael that I did not really listen to what was being said. My smile and good mood were about to change. I began to feel very confused. I asked my escort what was going on and he replied, "Nothing!" He looked as bewildered and confused as I felt. Then he muttered, "I don't know. They just asked me to go back to our original entrance." Later, I realized that my escort was too kind to reveal what was really said because he did not want to hurt my feelings. In time, I found out the missing words in the puzzle.

As we walked back to the other side of the stage, I was so dumb founded over what had just happened that I could barely focus on what we were doing. My cue finally arrived and I started to walk towards the stage then someone said, "No! No! Not yet!" I stopped in my tracks. Then someone said, "O.K. Go!" I felt the warmth of the glowing spotlight hit me and sensed the surprise of the audience as they yelled and applauded. I was so nervous and I kept thinking about possibly dropping the award. I thought please, T, do not drop this award whatever you do. The award was heavy and I remember wondering how much it actually weighed. No one warned me before hand that it was going to be heavy and it felt to be at least forty or fifty pounds. It was obvious that the award was too heavy for me – you could see the strain in my arms as I carried it. Somewhere in the back of my mind, I remembered the few awards I had won when I was a little child; one for gymnastics and one for a limbo contest. But that was kid stuff and this was the big leagues. Award shows and awards themselves did not get any grander then this event and I was presenting an award to the world's greatest star. I loved and adored Michael and I was once again participating in the making of his history.

As I stood before Michael, he was smiling. I stretched out my hands to honor him with his award and to relieve myself of its weight. When he took the award out of my hands, he walked to the microphone to begin his speech. At one moment when the audience was applauding, he turned to me and told me how surprised and happy he was to see me and that he'd had no idea that I was going to be there. I flinched in response and said, "Oh really? I was told you knew." My response jumped out of me spontaneously and I did not even have a chance to think about what I was going to say. He turned back to the microphone and towards the audience to finish his speech. I thought he was behaving strangely but did not quite know why. Somehow, I just felt Michael was not being sincere. He was not being honest with me somehow but I could not imagine why. I stood on stage near Quincy Jones and the Executive Producer of the show, Mr. Sidney Miller.

Michael's speech ended and he walked off stage and left me behind. I just stood there dumbfounded and numb. The audience showed their disapproval as they echoed a series of oooohhs and ahhhhhs. They broke my trance. This was not a televised event but if it had been, perhaps he would not have left me on the stage alone. I found it especially odd since he had just expressed how surprised and happy he was to see me. Yet, here he was leaving me on stage as I was following behind him. It just did not add up or make any sense to me.

Once we passed the curtains, out of view of the audience, his security surrounded him quickly — as if they were shielding him from all who tried to approach him. Before I knew it, I could no longer see him in view and he was gone.

Outside the theater, I saw the large trailer that was set up for him;

roped off by his security team. I spotted Mr. Brown and waited with him. I told him how badly I wanted to speak to Michael and how he had been rushed away before I could even talk to him. Ben encouraged me and told me to go for it! I mustered up all the power and determination within me and I told myself that I was not going to let this opportunity slip through my hands. I was within feet of him and I had to fight for this moment. I had to talk to him and let him know how I felt. I needed to find out why I was fired from the tour. What had I done to deserve that? Why did Sheryl Crow replace me? I just had to try to find out the answers or die doing so.

When I approached his trailer, I had butterflies in my stomach. I was far more nervous than I had been on stage with him. I had all the words that I wanted to say running rapidly through my head. I approached the gate and I asked Bill Bray, Michael's assistant, if he could please relay to Michael that I would like a moment with him. He told me that he would see what he could do.

While I stood there, Alfonzo Ribiero and Ricky Shroeder also waited to see Michael. Ricky was the child star from the sitcom *Silver Spoons*. I talked to them for a minute and before I knew it, they were admitted inside Michael's trailer.

After around ten minutes Alfonzo and Ricky came out of the trailer where I was still left feeling very alone. I stood there starring at Bill Bray patiently but I felt like some sort of peasant. I felt like something less than a peasant. Before I knew it, Bill yelled, "Well, Hurry up! If you are coming, come on! We do not have all day! We've got another award to get." I stood looking at him stunned and shocked. I just could not believe he was talking to me like that. I turned back to look at Mr. Brown to see if he had seen this. I just could not believe how he spoke to me in front of everyone that was there. He spoke to me as if I were trash. Yet, Alfonzo and Ricky were greeted so nicely. I was so embarrassed and humiliated that I wanted to cry. However, there was simply no time for tears.

Here was my moment, my long awaited cue, and I was going to get some questions answered from Michael.

When I walked towards Bill, I passed the entrance gate and the door to Michael's trailer flung open. I assumed and imagined that I would go inside the trailer to talk to him. That is what I hoped for anyway, but Michael walked out of his trailer and he stood before me. He kept repeating exactly the same words to me that he said on stage, as though he had been scripted. He said, "Oh Tatiana! It is so good to see you! I had no idea you were going to be here." It was like an instant replay, and it was so weird. I said, "Michael I would really like to talk to you." Right after I said that, Bill Bray grabbed Michael's arm and pulled him away saying, "We gotta go!" They did this as if they planned it. It reminded me of what Majestic told me about Michael always having other people bail him out of situations that he did not want to be a part of. Basically, Michael did not want to look like the bad guy. Michael closed with, "Oh well! I gotta go, sorry!" I just stood there in shock, and once again, I was alone. Obviously, he did not want to talk to me but I was being treated so disrespectfully for no valid reason. Why would Michael not let me talk to him? Why did he keep repeating the same comment to me? Why did he leave me on the stage alone? The biggest question was why did he tell me that he had no idea that I was going to be there, when he did know? The producer told me that he was aware of the entire show including the monologue. I was feeling very uncomfortable in my own skin, embarrassed and rejected. I told myself that it was time for me to move on. I turned around and I walked back towards Mr. Brown. Even though I felt ridiculous and stupid, I tried to carry myself with complete and utter confidence. I tried to regain my dignity, self-respect, and composure. I was speechless for a while, but I felt as though Ben sensed my pain and disappointment. I told Ben that I did not get a chance to speak to Michael and, of course, he had seen the entire thing. He knew what I was feeling and what really happened. Ben and I went back into the theater to watch the rest of the show. I heard someone whisper as I walked to my seat, "Ooooh…There she is!" Hearing the worst in that statement, I wanted to go home.

TR: What happened when you did go home?

TT: My girlfriends tried to help me make sense of it all but there was no comfort to be found. For the next two weeks, this disturbed me. I kept searching for answers within myself and I could not stop crying.

TR: Did you talk to Mr. or Mrs. Jackson about what happened at the award show?

TT: I told Mr. and Mrs. Jackson about my experience and that I did not get a chance to speak to Michael or get any of my questions answered. I explained the Bill Bray story, how he had spoken to me, and how I had been treated. Joseph made a remark about Bill that made it obvious that he disliked Bill and said that had he been at the awards with me none of that would have happened; I would have been able to speak with Michael. Katherine also said that she did not trust Bill. I remember asking myself what possible good their comments would do for me now. Perhaps they were in the dark but I felt as though they knew more than they were telling me.

TR: Did you speak to Ingrid about the show?

TT: Ingrid called to thank me for being a part of the show and she apologized for the way I had been treated. I knew at the time of the show it was perhaps obvious to others that Michael did not want to talk to me but now it was confirmed. I answered her with a question, "How I was treated?" I wanted her to verify it for me. She said, "I saw what happened and I felt really bad for you, having to go through all of that. I don't know what happened to you on tour but I heard a lot of different things and felt there were other people around Michael trying to keep you out. I thought I could help you two get together so you could talk." Ingrid said that she just really wanted to help and she was sorry how the whole thing turned out and how badly Michael had treated me. My curiosity grew when she admitted she was aware of the cold treatment I received. I felt that she knew more and my instincts were correct. I begged her to tell me what she knew and it took a lot of coaxing before she did. I said that whatever she had to tell me would not hurt me anymore than I have already been hurt. She finally told me that as she had been organizing the event she called Michaels publicist, Bob Jones. He told her that he had some concerns about me being involved with the presentation. She told me his comment was, "Tatiana, she's only a dancer! Why is she involved in it? Is she going to speak? Does she have anything to say?" Ingrid told me that she said, "No! She is just going to be presenting him with the award." He asked her, "Why does she have to be in it at all?" Ingrid told me that she reasoned with Bob and that she stated that because we had worked together before it would be a nice moment in the show and that the audience would enjoy this as well.

When I worked with Michael, it not only catapulted my career and brought me into the public eye but it helped his image. To some degree, it validated his masculinity to those who doubted it and fans often said that we were the perfect match and a believable pair.

Ingrid continued to explain the situation to me adding that Bob decided that they would go along with the idea as long as I was to present and not speak. It really hurt me to think that Bob Jones said such a thing about me when he did not even know me. Ingrid's information was enlightening. What I learned was that Michael knew that I was involved with the show, yet he had said repeatedly that he was surprised to see me and that he had no idea I was going to be there. My instinct that his sincerity was not real was correct. I hated to believe this. Oh, how I hated it, but it was true. He knew of my involvement and he even approved it, as long as I did not, "have anything to say." Ingrid also shed some light on the walkie-talkie incident that occurred when I was being escorted from behind stage left to stage right. I learned that the missing words to the puzzle were "Michael does not want to see or speak to Tatiana before the show." I knew that these words were probably true because I was rushed back to the opposite side of the stage from where he was to make his entrance. Then, when Bill Bray was pulling him away from me, it proved that they timed it so Michael would not have to deal with me. The entire thing was obvious to everyone.

TR: How did you feel after the phone call with Ingrid once you found out the truth?

TT: I cannot even put into words the devastation that I felt. It was very difficult to get over the pain that this and other experiences working with Michael had caused me. I never, in my wildest dreams, ever considered I could go through such agony. Looking from the outside in, you picture things so differently. I did anyway. At the time, I was so absorbed in it all and I wanted nothing more than to find answers. I look back on Ingrid as a beautiful spirit for trying to help me.

TR: Did you talk to anyone else about your experience at the award show?

TT: Majestic came over to visit me and we talked about it for hours. I told him everything and I took him through every part of the evening. Majestic explained again how Michael's people take the blame and they cover for him so he does not look like the one at fault. "He will not look like a bad guy," Majestic said. He reminded me of a similar experience that he had with Michael years prior when he visited him on a video shoot. Majestic helped me understand what really happened to me that night. He said that when Bill Bray yelled for me to "Come on," that he was probably giving Michael a cue for him to come outside his trailer so that I could not go inside. Then, when Bill pulled his arm saying, "We gotta go," that was also a planned skit. He made it clear to me that Michael did not want to speak to me. Just as David Banks pointed out before, if Michael wanted something, he got it! "What Michael wants, Michael gets," he said. It was naïve of me to think otherwise. Majestic reminded me that his own family complained about not being able to get in touch with him when they wanted. Majestic said, "Tatiana! Who do you think is to blame or really in control?" Our conversation opened my eyes some. It explained the crazy experience I just had but it still didn't answer the big and main question. Why? Why was I made to endure all of this? What had I done to be treated this way? These were the questions no one could answer. Only Michael knew exactly why I was fired from his tour. Only he could answer the questions about replacing me with his back-up singer.

I brought up the issue of not being paid for his 1988 calendar or the single's cover of *The Way You Make Me Feel.* Majestic said, "People just fuck you in this town and don't kiss you first, huh Tatiana?" He ended that wonderful comment with laughter, but it wasn't funny to me. This was my life and my career we are talking about. I still felt as though I was the underdog and wanted so badly to talk to Michael. I just couldn't help but feel that someone had filled his head with lies or something. Maybe he did not like the fact that I didn't audition for the *Dirty Diana* video. Somehow, I reason he had been lied to. He had the wrong impression of me.

Even after all the confusion and pain I endured from the experience of the B.R.E Awards Show, I still sent him a birthday gift three months later. It was August 1989 and I was making arrangements with Katherine to have it delivered. It was a huge, larger than life, full size portrait of his friend and idol. Marlon Brando. The portrait was from one of his classic films, *The Wild Ones*. It was a creation by my friend and artist, Demetrie Kabbaz. Jermains wife, Margaret, picked it up from me and we loaded it into her Jeep. At 3 ? feet wide and standing at 5'6" – 5'6"1/2 tall, it wasn't an easy gift to carry or transport.

TR: Did Michael call or send a thank you note for the gift?

TT: I never received a word of thanks or a card of gratitude. I was forced to realize that I was fighting a losing battle. I was beginning to tell myself that I just needed to move on! My heart was beyond broken. I endured more pain than anyone could ever comprehend or imagine and I felt so alone. The worst part was when fans or people approached me to ask me questions about him or the tour. I could not escape it all and I was constantly reminded of my private pain. I even went through a phase where I hated being me. I hated questions or comments like, "Hey, aren't you that girl from the Michael Jackson video? So, what is he like? Is he gay?" I would just cringe when I was bombarded with all the questions. I sometimes wished that I was someone else. I wished I had a new identity altogether. I even tried changing my image to get away from the comparisons. One time, I cut my hair very short – boy- short. I dyed it with blond streaks but none of that mattered. I was still recognized. I was even recognized when I wore sunglasses and a baseball cap pulled down low. When two young girls recognized me at the mall they said, "We could tell it was you because of your nose and that profile. Your look is striking." One of my closest friends, Eddie De Harp, always teased me and said, "T! Maybe you should have plastic surgery to get away from his look. Even though it really is your look." We laughed about how silly that sounded but yet how truthful the statement was. Ironically, Michael continued to change his face and his image into what was my natural look.

When I considered having surgery to change my image, I thought about it for a second and then the thought was gone. I don't do doctors. Just the thought of going under the knife turns my stomach.

TR: How do you feel about other people who get plastic surgery and the changes that Michael has surgically made to himself?

TT: If someone does not like the way they look and if they feel that surgery can help them with their self-esteem, then I say, "Go for it!" My motto is, "To each his own." Everyone has the right to live and choose as they please.

As for all the changes Michael has gone through surgically, I cannot help but feel sadness that something or someone caused him to feel inadequate, when to me he was always beautiful. I loved him during every stage of his life, even when he was on the Cher show performing with his brothers to their hit song *Dancing Machine*. They stood side by side doing the robot, which was a popular dance back then. They had the biggest afro's at the time. There was a made for T.V movie titled *The Jacksons- An American Dream*. This movie portrayed Michael when puberty was setting in and it started to affect his skin. Like most teens, he endured the horror of seeing his skin covered in acne. On top of that, he was constantly teased and taunted about his wide nose. People sometimes do not realize the damage they may cause with words alone. When I was a kid there was a saying, which I think we have all heard, "Sticks and stones may break my bones, but words can never hurt me." I remember always thinking that this was such a stupid and untrue statement because words do hurt. I think that in some cases, words can last a lifetime. Pain is not always physical.

When Michael and I did the video, I thought he was absolutely gorgeous and I was highly attracted to him. I never thought to myself that he would continue to alter his appearance. There was also a time when I agreed with people that we did look alike. There was a great resemblance. Now I look at Michael and I no longer see the guy I once worked with. He has changed almost beyond my recognition.

TR: Did you want to keep working, modeling, and acting after all that happened?

TT: I was going out less and less on auditions. I was in an odd position. I was in this sort of "catch 22" thing. I was looked at as somewhat of a celebrity but I was not a big enough name and my credits were not building. Everywhere I went the fans knew my name but the casting agents just couldn't seem to get past the quote, unquote, "Michael Jackson

Girl" thing. I finally did score a commercial for Miller Light.

On the day of the shoot, I was told that the director decided to put me in the background for fear that I would outshine or steal the thunder from the commercial's star, comedian Dennis Miller. It seemed as if I was a big enough star to threaten the stars status but I was not a big enough star to have my own campaign. This was the only offer I had at the time and when the commercial aired, I could not be seen at all. It was truly an odd position to be in and, strangely, many people that had been in the business for years envied me. So many artists are truly talented — they work for years on one project and then another and they do not get the recognition that was bestowed upon me from just one video. The thought of being employed on a regular basis in our industry without anyone knowing who I was sounded great to me. Here some actors envied me and here I was envying them. I thought I would be great on a soap opera because I had already been through so much drama and confusion that I was living my very own day and nighttime drama. I wondered if Michael's last video girl, Ola Ray, from *Thriller* ever experienced anything similar to my situation. I thought it would have been great to sit down, talk with her, and trade stories.

TR: How were you feeling emotionally at this time?

TT: I cried enough to make my very own river. I did not know what or who to believe. It was difficult for me to trust anyone. I could not even trust my own judgment anymore. Even the guys I dated made me feel like they were with me because of some celebrity status. Suddenly, I became this hot trophy. I could tell I was looked at as some kind of sex object. Real relationships were becoming difficult to find, male or female. I even questioned the friends I had prior to my 'newfound fame'. I mean, one of them stole the powder compact that Michael used while I was on tour with him. That was a hard pill to swallow. This so-called "friend" and I had a three-year friendship before all of the Hollywood crap. It really hurt me.

TR: You had to have at least one true friend out there…

TT: My friend, Valerie Simpson, took on the roll of a surrogate mom. She endured all the tears, confusion, and pain with me. I thanked God for her constantly. It was a blessing that I had someone as beautiful and compassionate as Valerie for my friend. Especially since my mom lived in Florida and she could only be supportive and compassionate by telephone. Valerie was my closest confidant and will forever be considered my "Guardian Angel" on earth during those times of despair. She saw it all, heard it all, and lived it all with me. I sometimes feel that if it were not for her love and support I would not have lived to tell this story. There were many times I considered ending it all. Not only was my heart broken but I also I had issues with working, dating, my own camp, and paying my rent. Many people assumed that I was set for life financially because I worked with the world's greatest entertainer of our time. No one could fathom the idea that I lived in a studio apartment and I did not have a car. Most people assumed that I was too big a star to be living like I was. When I went on dates, I would get picked up at my apartment and some guys could not believe that I did not own my own home. Many wondered why I was not driving around in a Mercedes. I once had a date with Kato Kailin (famous from the O.J. Simpson trial) and when he picked me up, he remarked, "This is where you live?" This was coming from a guy who lived as someone else's fricken house guest. At least I had my own place! Well, I never said that I always had the greatest taste in dates or men.

Even though times were difficult, I did not want to give up. I kept pursuing the Hollywood dream and continued to be knocked down, only to stand up and brush myself off repeatedly. I considered going overseas to work but decided not to go. I probably should have considered it more seriously.

TR: Did you ever have to ask anyone to help you financially?

TT: Michael's mother was aware of my hard times and she once gave Majestic fifty dollars to give to me. I sincerely felt that Katherine cared very much about me and was perhaps frustrated that she could not do more to help or to get Michael with me to talk. Yet, I could not understand why she did not ever make it happen. I guess it was too hard for her to do.

I had moved on from Joseph and the contract. I spent a lot of unnecessary time worrying about getting out of it, when in fact it was a null and void situation. None of the obligations were fulfilled within our agreement so I had nothing to worry about. It reminded me of the movie, *The Wizard of Oz*. Dorothy fretted so much about getting back home, when all the while she had never really left home. Here I was fretting about getting out of a contract that was not valid anyway. Ultimately, we went our separate ways without any complaint or argument.

TR: Was Joe Jackson upset that you did not want him to represent you any longer?

TT: Not at all, and it did surprise me a bit that Joseph didn't care enough about it to even discuss our parting ways. I did not accomplish anything at all during the duration of our contract. I even took several steps backward when I signed with him. None of the promises he or Katherine made to me were kept. They did not give me any answers about why I was fired and going to Neverland never happened. My disappointments were ongoing, but never did I complain to either one of them. I just accepted these losses and went on my way. I was under pressure, too, because the statue of limitations for the calendar and the 45 of *The Way You Make Me Feel* were almost over and the day was approaching that I would not be able to challenge Michael in court. I did not want to sue my idol but I couldn't help but feel like I was a casualty or some sort or a victim of circumstance. I was pleased that my contractual agreement with Joe Jackson ended amicably.

In 1991, I traveled to the Far East to resume working with Satoru, an agent I had worked with years before. This was when I ran into Rebbie Jackson again. We spent a few days together talking, having dinner, and site seeing during our time off. She was touring and promoting her album at the time. Although things did not go well with Joseph seeing Rebbie was like running into a family member.

When I returned to L.A for work, things still did not pick up for me. By this time, I did not have representation for management. I did not trust people anymore. I had made some awful choices and trusted the wrong people. Perhaps I had even missed out by letting the good ones slip through my hands. My brother William once told me, "If you know how to play the game of chess then you'll know how to play the game of life." I regret not knowing this game because I believe there is something to this theory. I believe this is simply what life is all about. Living and learning, if you haven't learned anything from it then you haven't lived. I look back now and see just how gullible and naïve I was about certain things and people in L.A. I was raised by teachers and I spent my formative years in New York City. I thought I had learned a bit about street smarts. Still I had yet to learn a thing or two about Hollywood and its smoke and mirrors. Many people play games there. There is a difference in New Yorkers. They are not fake with you. They are straight up and honest to the core, which I adore. But in L.A people can be very plastic and pretentious in many ways. Not everyone, but many that I met. Hollywood is a city that is made up of dreams and fairy tales. If you are not strong within your beliefs and convictions, you can lose your soul there. I did not loose my beliefs or my soul, but I did loose some of the magic and wonderment that I had when I first arrived there. Auditioning even changed for me because I started to question my own ability and talents. I felt as though I was not in the moment when I was auditioning, as if I were outside myself — judging me. Like some kind of outer body experience. I lost myself due to all the deception.

Working with my idol took me through many experiences. I knew what it was like to go from anonymity to suddenly being 'famous' within just a few days. I anticipated doors being opened but in the end, no one even acknowledged my knock. They would not even give me work as an extra. I did not have any prior knowledge of the entertainment business and I found myself flat broke. Having a good support system is a big advantage. The people that are behind you and backing you, both professionally and personally are very important. The message behind the movie *Mahogany* is so true. "Success is nothing without someone to share it with."

To top it all off, I lost a different loved one each year for three years. I endured endless pain. As each person in my life passed on, I in turn, lost strength and energy. As soon as I would regain my strength and start to feel better, another one left me.

TR: Who were the important people in your life that you lost?

TT: In 1989, I lost my mentor, Svengali Antonio Lopez. I felt in many ways that if it were not for him, I never would have made it as far as I did. He gave and taught me so much about the industry. I take great pride in being an "Antonio Girl." Not many hold the title and the ones that do are of an elite few. Some of the others are Jessica Lange, Pat Cleveland, Jerry Hall, Grace Jones and Toukie Smith –are all Antonio's girls. Losing Antonio was devastating to me. He was like my brother, my father, my teacher, my friend, and my everything wrapped up in one. I miss him dearly.

In 1990, I lost my one and only link to this life itself, my biological mother. This was one of the most difficult burdens for me. Although I have two wonderful parents who are there for me, a biological mother is incomparable as far as people and relationships are concerned.

In 1991, I lost my closest male friend and my soul mate, Chanti Gani Tyrus, a.k.a. Eric Tyrus. He was truly one of a kind. I will always consider losing him a great-great loss. He was everything to me! Someday I will tell the story of our lives together.

TR: How did you manage without representation?

TT: In 1992, I became my own Agent/Manager and I put together a package and proposal for *Playboy* Magazine. There was much interest and I came close to signing with them. Considering the deal made me reflect on my *Bad Tour* days when Miko and I debated the future and if I would ever consider a *Playboy* spread especially if I was paid the right price. But at this point in my life, it wasn't just about the paycheck. It was more about having new opportunities. I looked at it as a chance to have a voice and to be taken to the next level professionally. I felt that perhaps it should be the next step in my career, but the deal did not happen.

TR: Why? What happened?

TT: One of Hugh Hefner's assistants told me that Hef was a good friend of Michael's and that he did not want to involve himself with anything that was not "Pro-Michael Jackson." Never did I consider my story to be against Michael in any way. If anything, my story was that of a woman who cared very much about him. However, because I was fired from his tour people thought that I must have been on bad terms with him. I began to realize that it was an old issue and that no one in the industry cared to hear about it, but the fans did want to know what happened. I was constantly bombarded with Michael Jackson questions. I felt so stifled and frustrated not having a verbal outlet. I convinced myself that

I was better off not doing *Playboy*. That somehow I was being saved from something that really was not meant to be, that someday I would have my voice heard, and I would finally be at peace with it all.

Chapter Nine
Supporting The Bad One

In early 1993, the world was in shock. One day, I walked into my L.A mom Valerie's apartment. She asked me with such seriousness, "Did you hear the news?" I replied, "Hear what news?" I sat down. The news was on every television channel, and repeated throughout the day. Valerie explained the events, and I was horrified. I could not believe what I was hearing. The news was reporting that Michael was being accused of molesting the little boy that accompanied him throughout his travels. I was too horrified to speak. I just could not believe what I was hearing. I was torn with emotions about the whole issue and subject. My heart went out to Michael and the pain he might have been enduring. Even though I had been subjected to so much turmoil, confusion, frustration, and mental anguish, I still cared. I still had compassion left for him in my heart. Somehow, I could not allow myself to believe that this Peter Pan Humanitarian could commit such an awful crime or act on a child. He did so much good for all children around the world. It was beyond my comprehension. I became caught up in the daily news stories and reports, and I could not help but feel pity for him. I could not fall asleep some nights thinking about him and his well-being.

TR: Did you think the allegations were true?

TT: I did not know what to believe. However, I chose to believe in his innocence. It was too difficult a pill to swallow. I could not think that he was guilty of harming a child. After all, caring about children was a large part of his image.

My friend Chris Ameruoso encouraged me to express my support for him publicly. Initially, the thought frightened me, but I did consider doing it. I thought it would be good for him to know that I was still in his corner. Also, the public would see that I was.

TR: Why did the idea of you expressing your support frighten you?

TT: I was frightened at the thought of the issue itself. This was a serious implication. Nevertheless, my love for Michael and my belief in him gave me the willpower and strength to go forward with my pursuit, and to speak out on his behalf.

Chris set up my first interview on the *Howard Stern Radio Show*. I remember being nervous because I did not know much about Howard until the day before our call. I did not know what to expect or if he was going to be kind to me. I was not knowledgeable about his show and I just did not know what to expect. It's a strange experience to have so many people hear you speak to someone by phone that you've never met. It's so cold and impersonal. You cannot see that person's expressions or see what is in his or her eyes. If you cannot see into a person's eyes, you are not connecting with their soul.

When Chris handed the phone to me, Gary, the producer of Howard's Show, asked me questions about the video shoot to confirm I was the girl. My heart raced, and Howard welcomed me. He was straight to the point. He then asked the question that was on everyone's mind. "Did you sleep with him? What proof do you have that he is a heterosexual." Suddenly my being in support of his innocence meant having to offer personal information about my intimacy with the pop star. I took offense to this fact, yet at the same time, I wished that I did have some proof for people. In my heart, I felt that I had enough proof. I was not as prepared as I thought I was for such a strong and opinionated host as Howard Stern. Howard left me with something to think about when he asked me, "I don't get why you're in support of him. Why the loyalty?" I knew he had a point and it made me question myself. It was a great question and there was no clear reason why I supported Michael, other than wanting to believe in his innocence and loving him dearly. Because of the love and adoration I had for Michael, he could do no wrong in my eyes. By nature's course, I am a Taurus who is ruled by Venus. This means that I am stubborn, determined, diligent, and in-love with the thought of love itself. The sign Taurus believes in loyalty and they will endure anything and put up with a lot before they give up and let go of something or someone. It is hard for them to move on. Howard could not have conceived just how much I had gone through. It was a tough interview, but overall, Stern was pleasant to me and his partner Robin impressed me. She knew all of my credits, which she read aloud. This was the best and the hardest interview of them all.

My next interview was for Black Entertainment Television. It was a one on one piece with the reporter and it helped that I could see her eyes. I was emotional, and I was honest and the words came from my heart. The interview caused me to lose control and cry on camera. I hated that but it was real. If truth be told, I was optimistic and I thought that perhaps this would bring Michael and me together. Maybe he would see just how much I cared and loved him.

About a week later, I was in touch with Katherine and Joseph. I expressed my concern and sincere support. I could tell that they were somewhat surprised that I was in support of him. I reassured them that I was not taking a stand for any payment. I just wanted to show my support.

There was another interview scheduled. It was in New York City for *The Maury Povich Show*. On the panel, I found myself among people who were in support of the pop star and people who were not. Majestic was in the group of Michael supporters with me. I found it a bit surprising that neither Joseph nor Katherine made an appearance. They commented by telephone. Nevertheless, I knew that it was all taking a toll on them and their health. They were both disturbed by it all and who wouldn't be? This was there baby and these were serious allegations. It was nothing to take lightly.

TR: What questions were you asked at this interview?

TT: They asked me similar questions Howard Stern asked me on his radio show. "Did the two of you have sex?" That was all anyone was concerned about and that is what they wanted an answer to. As if my saying we had, was going to validate his manhood; that my affirmation would have made him innocent of these horrific accusations. I do so wish that I could have told them that we did have sex, but if we did, how was I to prove this to the public or media? I wished I could have gone beyond just speaking out on his behalf, but I could not. I had already blurted out something about us dating for close to a year and I said that we were romantically involved when in fact we were not. There were only a few visits to the set of *Leave Me Alone* and *Baby Bad*. Even though I had old issues lingering in the back of my head, I put them all aside for the sake of love and loyalty. As I told even one little white lie I was becoming a part of it all.

TR: So you lied and said that you dated Michael for a year when you did not? Why did you do that?

TT: The lie slipped out of my mouth simply because of my feelings for him. I felt that an injustice was being committed. Plus, I wanted Michael to see how much that I loved him. In my fairytale mind, I thought that he would come looking for me to thank me. Boy was I wrong!

I regretted being on the panel at the Maury show. It was all about debate and somehow I just did not foresee it being that way. I was there as a supporter, not as a judge and jury. However, for many people, that was not good enough. Some on the other panel were security guards that had worked for the Jacksons, at their Hayvenhurst home. In fact, some were involved in a lawsuit against the Jacksons. They told stories about Michael and his young male guests at the house. Suddenly, I was out of my realm. I did not have anything to say about this topic. The panelists were arguing saying that I never visited the house when Michael still lived there, and they were right! I became a visitor after he moved out. I had to remind myself that I was there to support Michael, not to lie.

When I blurted out something about dating Michael his mother Katherine confirmed his feelings and love for me and it angered the other panel guests because they were trying to crucify him. It was an odd situation that I put myself in the middle of, yet I was still willing to go to war for him. I could only imagine the mental and physical stress he was going through.

TR: How did you feel when you saw Michael on television at this important time?

TT: The CNN piece stunned me. Michael was looking straight into the camera. He was dressed in a red shirt, donned false eyelashes, and he was claiming his innocence. I felt that if there was any moment and time that Michael needed to look a little more normal and down to earth, this was the time to do it. He needed to show every aspect of his masculinity. I was angry when I thought about it wondering why he wasn't being better advised. This was such a critical and serious time. If he was going to come clean and talk to the media about this, then he needed to look the part as well. I pitied him and felt he was not getting the best advice. I wanted to help him and I felt as though there was an injustice being committed. I just could not see Michael harming a child. In my heart of hearts, I knew that when we worked together on the video, there were real sparks and feelings between us. The feelings were mutual. His own mother confirmed this fact.

TR: Do you think it may be possible that his mother just wanted to believe that he was in love with a woman? Is it possible that she wanted others to believe this as well to protect her son?

TT: You are asking me if she could have been in denial about his sexuality. When I think about all the little flirtations, gestures, and looks he gave me, I just cannot fathom that none of that was true or real. I am convinced he did feel something for me at one time. I mean real feelings, and if he was gay, well, I would probably have still loved him anyway.

I went back to Los Angeles and I continued in my fight and support for Michael. I wrote a letter to Oprah hoping that she would do a story with me and perhaps some other women who had worked with him. However, no such luck.

Soon I was horrified by an interview his sister La Toya gave at a live press conference. She said something to the effect of, "I cannot and will not stand by and allow little innocent children to be hurt by my brother, and I won't be a silent collaborator to this." This was so shocking to say the least. Like many of us, I could not believe his own sister was speaking against him yet I feared there was truth to what she was saying. After all, she is his flesh and blood and we assume that family knows their own. This of course, is not always the case. At any rate, her statements certainly did not help him.

Then it was soon reported that Michael settled with the boy for around twenty million dollars. I was sad because I knew how this was going to make him look. The world would think that he was guilty. I was also disappointed because I believed he was going to fight to the end to prove his innocence. I was disappointed on both sides of the coin. Both sides came out looking bad.

I had also hoped that my defending him would bring us close. I at least wanted some kind of contact, but once again, I never heard from Michael. He did not even send me a thank you card. I did not understand why he shut me out. I believed in him. My friend, Iris Parker, kept telling me to wake up and smell the coffee. She said that it was time for me to move on for good.

TR: Why do you think Michael should he have sent you a thank you card?

TT: It's not that he had to thank me for supporting him. It just would have been a polite thing for him to do. No matter what, I did it because I believed in him, and wanted him to know it. I will never regret my support and love for him. However, I secretly hoped that he would reply.

Chapter Ten
The Star Stinks

I had an opportunity to tell my story to the *Star* Magazine. I do not regret it because I learned a lot about dealing directly with the tabloid world. They did more than misquote me, they wrote:

"The Writing Was On the Wall. I knew that when Michael started hanging around with a boy the stories would start. He liked the kid so much I heard he gave his family a million dollars, fancy clothes, exotic vacations and a Rolls-Royce. He made it clear he preferred the kid's company to mine, but when I read he paid out so many millions to the little boy in the sex abuse case, while still protesting his innocence, it somehow had a hollow ring. It was as if he wanted people to think he was an all American, red-blooded male. That one-day he would find a mate, get married have kids. That I would have his babies, when deep down in his heart he knew he never would."

This paragraph was total bullshit! It was not even funny! My own mother knew and said, "That wasn't you speaking, I can tell that. You do not even speak like that." More than eighty percent of the story was the writer's words added in. The writer was speaking for me, and he was putting words in my mouth.

I told them the story about Michael taking a little boy and his family shopping, but the press had already reported that. Everyone had already heard that story. Everything else the writer added made me want to puke. However, it did teach me a great lesson about tabloids. They are trash. I was so ticked off by it all. They want to exaggerate stories to feed to the curious. They even lie if they have to. Sadly, I was not only hurt by this piece but learned a great lesson from the experience. I still had more than I realized to learn. Some people asked me about the story and they wanted to know why I did it. They made me feel like I was guilty of something.

TR: Did you feel guilty after the piece came out?

TT: I did not feel guilty because I did not tell them that story. Those were not my words or my feelings. It was not my way of expressing myself and it was not the message I was trying to send out at all! In my mind, I did not feel a connection to it. It was simply someone else's words with my photo attached. However, it was too late. The damage was done.

TR: Did you speak to anyone about it? Did you let people know that it was not your words?

TT: I spoke with Majestic sometime after. He told me that Katherine was hurt by the piece and she did not like it. She had no idea just how much I hated it, too, and how twisted it was. I tried to explain my true intentions but it did not matter. What was done was done. My support of Michael had not brought me any closer to him or his family.

Sometime in May of 1994, Michael married Lisa Marie Presley, the King's daughter. Initially, I was stunned. I did not know what to think. My brain went blank.

TR: How did you feel when you heard the news?

TT: Honestly, it made me reflect on the *Star* story when they said; *"It's as if he wanted people to think he was an all-American, red blooded male. That one day he would find a mate, get married have kids, etc."* Blah! Blah! Blah! It appeared to me that he decided to do exactly what they sarcastically said he would not do. Who knows, maybe that piece inspired him to get married. Just maybe, whoever wrote the piece, knew that Michael harbored feelings for me at one time. Maybe this was their opportunity to kill and banish any possibility of us ever reuniting.

TR: Did you ever express to the writer of the *Star* story how you felt about him twisting your words?

TT: I did express to the writer that I was disappointed in the piece. I felt both sides looked bad and that I wished Michael well. Of course, they did not print that.

TR: Did you feel that Michael and Lisa Marie's marriage was conventional?

TT: After viewing Michael and Lisa's appearance on MTV and watching their famous kiss, well, all I have to say is, our kiss was far more convincing. The proof is in the picture, but she carried the name Mrs. Jackson. Even though all of this was odd for me, I wished them well. A part of me did question the union of these too, and I tried not to judge them.

TR: Did you wish it were you that married Michael instead of Lisa Marie?

TT: Yes, it hurt that it was not me. However, I put everything in the Lord's hands, because I trust in Him. For whatever the reasons, it was not meant to be. I believe in destiny and for some reason as much as I loved and adored Michael, something pushed us apart. I try not to regret anything, as there is something to learn in everything. You should not regret a lesson. Mistakes are blessings.

They are to learn from. Everything has a reason and a rhyme in life. My experience with the *Star* story made me feel like I had been used. I will never do another interview with them. Well, not unless the interviewer is Victoria Gotti. I will make an exception for her. I admire her and I think she is absolutely beautiful. I think she would be fair as a journalist. She is unlike some of the journalists out there who get a kick out of exaggerating things and putting words into someone's mouth. Therefore, I guess I should not say that I would never do a story with them again, because you never know!

Chapter Eleven
Once More Disappointed

In 1996, I wanted to seek out a book deal in hopes of getting my story out there. I wanted the true story to be told and I wanted it told in my words. I found a publisher who was interested in my story.

TR: Did you know the publisher or anyone at the publishing company?

TT: I did have an old acquaintance working there. It was Michael's ex-sister in-law, Margaret Maldonado; Jermaine's ex-wife. Again, I was destined for another Jackson scenario. They signed me immediately to a deal that was a follow up to a hot Hollywood tell all book. They titled my project *Once More with Feeling* which turned out to be more like, "Once More with Crap." Again, there were things printed in the book that I found were not correct and that I had not said. Also, the publishers omitted certain stories completely — especially my Michael Jackson experiences. It seemed that they became selective without consideration of the complete story I had to tell.

TR: Did you tell them that you wanted the story to be in your real words this time?

TT: Going into the deal, I was led to believe that I would be able to tell my stories and experiences. However, this was not true. It became clear to me that this was now their story, and it was going to be about what they wanted it to be about. I was one of five other authors. I was disappointed to the max. I think I was the only one who had any entertainment credits. All the others except myself and one other author involved, were call girls. When I think about it now, I should not have been involved with the project. I feel that I was in a different league all together. Unfortunately, I learned this a little too late. The other author with a legitimate story was Jennifer Young. She was born into showbiz royalty. She is the daughter of the Oscar winning actor, Gig Young.

During our book tour, it hit me. "What the hell am I doing here," I was sitting on a panel with prostitutes. "Will I ever get the proper forum to tell my story?" I was mad at myself for settling for this deal. That is exactly what I did, I settled! I did it because I thought that any deal was better than no deal, right? Not true! Sometimes it is better just to sit back and wait for the right one, and at the right time. I still had much to learn. I left my parents at the young age of fourteen to pursue a ballet scholarship. I was taught ballet, not the lessons and knowledge of deal making. Add to that the fact that I am very stubborn. Once I set my mind on something that is pretty much it. That is all she wrote! I go for it headstrong and headfirst.

TR: Do you think people thought you were a prostitute because you were involved with this book?

TT: Well, I was called a former prostitute once when I was doing an interview on a high profile show. I was in the camera shot and standing with some of the other authors, so some people will remember this as their impression of me.

I was disappointed in the entire project and it was not lucrative as one might think. I made no more than I did doing the video for Michael and to date, I have been paid no residuals. Unfortunately, I went for this book deal headstrong. I believed I would tell my story in the way that I wanted to. Knowing Margaret made the deal feel reassuring and I thought I was in good hands. It gave me a sense of comfort. Once again, I had no one to blame but myself. So, after being called "a former prostitute" on national television all I could feel was shame and guilt for possibly embarrassing my family and our name. I was far more concerned that I humiliated my parents. I worried more about them taking it to heart more than I did myself. I am a strong person and I have learned that you can't beat the masses. Some will dislike you, just to dislike you, no matter what!

Oddly though, as I found myself in this predicament, I reflect on my school days. When my father was a principal, I attended his school for one year. I was sent to the principal's office so many times that I remember my dad saying once, "We'll talk about it later at home." I was left with this feeling of "Oh, Oh, I did it again! I messed up, and I'm in trouble." I got myself into trouble so much that even Dad got tired of my shenanigans. It was never anything big that I got in trouble for. Just small, silly stuff. I was mostly guilty of not paying attention. I just was not listening, or I was thinking about something else. The lesson here is that I rushed into a project before thinking. I was just dying to be heard and to get my story out there. I wanted to express myself in my words. It has been hard for me to see articles and books that I have been affiliated with that have not done justice to my words in my story. They changed them to suit their needs. That hurt and angered me.

TR: So you take responsibility for mistakes made in your career?

TT: I have made my mistakes and I feel they were lessons bestowed on me by the Lord. I have learned from every one of them, and I will continue to do so with every new day that greets me with its smile and the joy of life itself.

It was a great disappointment from both of these projects, the *Star* and the book. I was forced and determined to do my own book in my own words. I do not want to leave this life knowing that I have been greatly misquoted. It would please me to know that I did it my way, Yah Know? You can only keep a bull down for so long. In no way are they to be messed with and like I said before, they can only take so much.

Since both of my last two disappointing projects I found discontentment in the land of make-believe. So I packed up in 1996, and I headed back home to Clearwater. I had a brief reunion with my family, then shortly afterwards I was on my way to South Beach, Miami. I have tried to live a normal life, distancing myself from showbiz and the entertainment world altogether. I have found that I have been blessed with the fact that I made an impression on people. It has been fifteen years and I've found daily, that at least one person still recognizes me and generally extends a warm greeting. I have even met people who told me that they named their child after me. That is incredible to me. To know that you've touched someone's life so much or inspired them somehow is just a phenomenal thing and great feeling. I cannot say that I still enjoy being bombarded with all the Michael Jackson questions. I have had fans who have echoed this sentiment to me. They would say that I was the luckiest girl in the world and all I could think to myself was, If they only knew! If they only knew the confusion, turmoil, stress, and pain. Could someone still consider this lucky?

I have moved on with my life. However, just hopefully this book - MY BOOK - will be the remedy to cure all curiosities. Perhaps it will answer some of the questions to those who wondered what happen to that girl they considered so lucky.

Chapter Twelve
The Last Word

You can never really know someone's life, until you have actually walked in their moccasins and lived their journey. I have learned so many lessons for one lifetime. I feel I have a few left over for the next life, if there is a next. Even though I endured a lot on this crazy roller coaster, I will admit I am lucky in the sense that I was able to see a childhood dream come true. For that, I am truly blessed. Perhaps, I am the one guilty for not knowing when to wake up from a dream. I also learned that you do not always find the answers to everything. Some things are simply meant to be a mystery, just like life. Still, it has been a wonderful ride. If I were to leave this planet earth tomorrow, I would say, "It's been an incredible journey filled with wonderful surprises and many blessings. I am grateful for every dream that I had that came true. I've been blessed with enough inspiration to want to continue the pursuit of my dreams." I haven't given up my interest of modeling and acting, and since the birth of the Internet, the idea of becoming my own boss, agent, and entrepreneur has tweaked my interest. It's enticing to think that for the first time in my career, I can decide and control things. I can call the shots. I can have artistic control, choose the photos, location, and create ideas. This is so enticing to me because I have been longing for an outlet in which to show my creativity.

Opposite:Tatiana Now!

In 2002, while living on South Beach, I could have continued my modeling career with one of the many agents in South Florida. I did sign with one of them. Somehow, I just could not get myself into the mentality of being one out of a possible hundred on the audition circuit again. Therefore, I never called in. I had already surpassed that goal; I already made a name for myself, and my friends and many people always reminded me of that. My look today has not changed much. People often tell me that I look the same, and I agree. God has been good to me.

Even though I failed to follow up with my agent on a day-to-day basis, I did photo shoots with a couple of different photographers on the beach. I wanted to create future shots for a website I dreamed about having someday.

One day I was shooting the breeze with my brother Harold over the phone. I told him about the new photos I was taking and how I had this great idea. I wanted to have my own website. He started telling me about some sites on the internet that already said that they had pictures of me on them. He found them just by typing my name in on a search engine. We discovered that several sites, with different domain names, claimed to have pictures of me inside their member's section. They were using my name to lure my fans there, but they did not have any pictures of me when you went to there sites. Most of them were celebrity porn sites. I was distressed and disturbed. I decided to hire an attorney to handle the matter.

He took my case, and soon after, we signed an agreement. He found my name on over fifty celebrity porn sites. I could not believe it. I was completely shocked. I was happy when I found out that they did not super impose my photo. They do that on some sites. I did feel like I was on the right track, but the webmasters beat me to the idea. This only inspired me more. I started to focus. I had to keep this dream alive, and continue my pursuit.

After about a month or so, I went to four lunch meetings with my new attorney. Each time, he went over the strength of my case and the millions we could make. Then suddenly, he dropped my case after I said that I would not join him for coffee one day. He had already made millions before meeting me, so money was not his objective. He was sharp, smooth talking, and always wore a suit. At every meeting we had together, he drove a different car. Each time he picked me up, the cars got fancier and fancier. He was just trying to impress me. The way he talked reminded me of several men in Los Angeles. He was the kind of guy that talked real big, full of hot air, and he was a shark. It was clear to me that I was his motive. I never bothered to find another attorney. Instead, I put my energy into my own project.

I finally found someone I connected with, creatively. I feel we share the same goals. I was working as a hostess in a popular South Beach restaurant and in walks a blonde bombshell named Tonia Ryan. When she walked in heads turned, tails wagged, and the claws came out. Right away, I liked something about her. Besides her obvious good looks, she appeared to be a very strong and a confident young woman. One who also seemed very secure with herself! Before I realized it, she became a regular at the restaurant. My closest co-worker at the restaurant introduced us. Greg told me, "OH, You've got to meet this girl Tonia! She has been coming in a lot lately and you two should meet. She's doing websites." Even though I was not sure what he meant at the time, because he is not internet savvy, he tweaked my curiosity. I wanted to meet Tonia.

When he introduced us, I was not a bit surprised. I knew that from the moment I met her, she was special. Somehow, I knew she would be a part of my future.

After our first meeting, it was obvious that we shared many of the same visions and ideas. We agreed that we are going to be successful entrepreneurs and that she and I would become a very strong team that people would take seriously. Tonia is extremely bright. Do not let her good looks fool you. She is a brain-iack.

Contrary to my background or beliefs she was, for many years, a feature dancer; the "main performer" in a strip club. A feature dancer travels around the country to appear and be billed as the star or the main attraction at the country's most successful strip clubs. To reach this position they must build credits being featured in adult magazines like *Playboy, Penthouse, Hustler,* etc.

Concluding her club career, Tonia moved to Las Vegas and became a very successful entrepreneur owning and operating a chain of high-end tanning salons. She attended UNLV and became a webmaster, and she now owns her own cosmetics line called, X-Girl Cosmetics. I applaud her for her strength and courage to do what she needed on her path and journey in life.

Me and Tonia Ryan

Opposite: Me and Tonia at the Delano Hotel in South Beach

In April 2003, the media reminded me, once again, that people are still interested and curious about what I am doing. The *British Broadcasting Company*, called me and so did the producers from the E Channel. Both channels wanted to do an interview with me because there was more breaking Michael Jackson news. The general broadcast media was airing clips and scenes from an up coming special about Michael; a two-hour piece shot at Neverland. The journalist was Martin Beshir and the piece seemed to backfire.

Michael did not come off in a good light. I do not think he was prepared for this. Sadly, the interview put him in a sorrowful and pathetic light. It appeared that Michael was completely out of touch with reality. I could not believe it. I felt it was a real calamity for him and a sad state of affairs. I somehow could not understand how this happened. How could Michael allow this to happen? I am not one to talk though. I am the first person who understands the concept of making mistakes and trusting the wrong people. It can happen.

Many people asked me why Michael did not hire me for our number during his Thirtieth Anniversary show. He hired Brittany Spears to do my part for the show. Many people said to me, "Yes, we like Britney Spears, but it would have been better to see you with Michael again. You are the original girl. The fans would have loved it." I will admit that I agreed with them. People would have been very pleasantly surprised to see us together again.

In September 2003, the BBC contacted me again. The interviewer said that she read about me in two books; Christopher Anderson's biography on Michael and a book titled, *FREAK*. *Freak* was from the files of the *National Enquirer,* and incorporated my story from the *Star* as their reference. That made three books, written about Michael that included me. The first was an unauthorized biography by of Michael by Randy Terraborelli. It is quite amazing that none of the authors contacted me. A legitimate writer quotes from a source but not these.

The days that I fell asleep thinking about Michael are long gone. *The Way He Made Me Feel* honestly, was confused and hurt. Professionally, Michael kicked me to the curb and exploited my image. He did this to me, and I did not reap any of the rewards. For some reason though, I will always have a soft spot for the one that captivated my eye. I saw him the first time when I was a young girl. Even though there are some people that debate his true interest and his real feelings for me, I will always beg to differ. Some people said that it was all a farce. Deep down, in my heart of hearts, I know there was a time that I had his heart too. What happened to that, or what changed it? I may never know. Only Michael himself holds all the answers. Maybe one day someone will ask him and he will answer.

Chapter "Lucky" Thirteen

The Lessons We Choose To Learn

Near the end of 2003, I received a surprise phone call from Majestic; I believe due to the BBC interest in using me in their story. The BBC, without my permission, passed him my number since Majestic and I have not spoken in nine or ten years. Once I recovered from the surprise of his call, he said "Joe and Katie said to tell you hello. They still love you and think about you. Michael also said to tell you hello. He said that he will call you as soon as he gets a chance. Then the two of you can get married, have babies, and live happily ever after." Then he started laughing. I questioned what he was saying to me. I asked him, "Excuse me, what did you say?" I asked him that just so he would repeat himself. He did, and he repeated it word for word. We both laughed. Then I replied sarcastically and I said, "Yeah sure Majestic, Whatever!" He said, "I haven't changed huh, Tatiana?" I completely agreed! Majestic is very aware that he is a jokester. I do admit though, I hoped that maybe there was some glimmer of truth that Michael was going to call me, but Majestic just planted this seed of deceit.

I found out a few days later, through the BBC, that they were with Majestic when he called me. I figured that he made this call for their benefit. It was nothing more, or nothing less. It was not surprising to me at all. I told the BBC, during my phone interview, the Jacksons were like a family to me. There was a time that I believed that and I was under that impression. Now, I can see clearly and I harbor no bad feelings. I just simply moved on.

On November 13th, 2003 as I was in Miami editing this book with my business partner, Tonia Ryan. The world was being barraged with breaking news about Michael. They were reporting an arrest warrant out for the pop star on several counts of child molestation charges. I wish I could say that I was shocked, but I cannot. I was not surprised, because he admitted in the Martin Beshure interview this year that he still has sleepovers with children. The situation is awful and it disgusts me that the media behaves like a pack of wolves ready to devour the meek. We say men are innocent until proven guilty, but we lie. We speak with forked tongues and enjoy taking pleasure in one's pain and weakness. There is such hypocrisy and judgment in our society and this saddens me so.

If there is truth to Michael's guilt in molesting a child, I feel he needs love, support, and above all, help! I am aware the media needs a good story, but enough is enough. I do not understand this need for crucifying someone repeatedly, and taking such pleasure in something so awful and negative. Even though Michael has changed before my eyes, all of our eyes, and he has a sad appearance, he still is a human being. He is a human being that needs help. I do not agree with how the media is playing this out.

It is a sad and pathetic display of humanity. Perhaps I am preaching my beliefs to those who do not believe or are unawake of God's love. We all answer for our sins eventually. For there is no greater judge and jury but the Lord. I will pray for Michael, whether he is innocent or not, and I wish him nothing but the best. I do not believe in an eye for an eye. I am no longer under his magical celebrity spell.

I also learned a lot about not idolizing him or any other human being. We are all equal. I can see with open eyes now. You can cloud your judgment of people if you look at them as celebrities instead of just looking at the person. I have seen fans that act as if Michael is a god. He is not! He is flesh and blood just like the rest of us. I have learned so much throughout this journey and I hope I continue to do so.

Only time will tell what the future will hold for me or for Michael, but after everything I still believe in my dreams. You can call me crazy, if you like, but I will always have a bit of a soft spot for the little kid from Gary, Indiana who captured my eye and made me a part of his history.

Burning Misery

Painting on this mask I'm naive to the journey that awaits me; greeted by other's, I find that there just as much a mystery. Angel's dance above me as I sing set my spirits free, for I have yet to see elements other than their lies and treachery. Living in a world of make believe mask faces and fantasies, really isn't all It's cracked up to be. For every mask never fails in lying to me. All I seek in their eyes is a truth and (above all) sincerity. Is that really too much to ask? I ask of Thee. God please! Spare me from this burning misery.

They judge me by things I have of no control, but powerless of this I'm not I know. Yet all this crazy madness is taking its toll. I plead to be released of this pain that has upon me a hold. I ask constantly, Is this really where I want to be? Because they speak with forked tongues bringing pain unto me. I came (they say) from under the deep blue sea, but fear I'm becoming jaded as one can be. Blinded long enough I want to be guided into the light, the greatest of all of ultimate height.

As I will continue to guard my soul, but no promises that it won't grow cold. It's been hard enough to trust those of power and greed, and sometimes those who are weak and in need. Spare me from this burning misery and guide me to a better plane. For my vulnerability remains the same, (Innocent like a child) and inevitably falling into more games. If anything, I guess that's what I would most like to change.

—Tatiana Y. Thumbtzen

(Drawing on the following page by Tatiana)

Neverlands Lost Boy
BadGirlT.Com

Printed in the United States
25431LVS00001BD/1-18